The BUMPER BUNBURY ALBUM

by David English
& Jan Brychta

Dedicated to Brian Johnston CBE, MC – a true Bunbury.

Illustration: *Jan Brychta*
Design Direction: *Bev Speight*
Design: *Nigel Wright*
Editorial: *Liz Dean, Deborah Kayser, Kerry Herbert*
Editor: *Mary Lambert*

Printed in Great Britain by
Scotprint Ltd, Musselburgh

OPENING OVER

Each year in aid of charity, the Bunburys play 20 cricket games for many worthy causes such as Mencap, Leukaemia Research, Childline, Multiple Sclerosis and other professional cricketers' benefits. Why do we, the Bunburys, do it?

Well, the celebrities enjoy themselves and have fun playing, the public enjoy watching them, and the proceeds go to a needy cause. So everybody wins.

So far, the Bunburys have raised £1.3 million for worthwhile ventures. They have appeared on TV, radio, video and CD. The Bunbury name is synonymous with cricketing fun everywhere.

Cricket is a sport that will always inspire youngsters throughout the world. Whether they're playing in the back streets of Bombay, on the beach in Barbados or on a perfect green pitch in England, their dream will be the same – to one day be good enough to play for their country. In 1996, many talented young players from around the world will get their chance as the Bunburys and the English Schools Cricket Association will stage the first ever Junior World Cup. This event will give the world's youngsters a chance to play the game at its highest level, to meet other nationalities, and to compete as part of a team against other talented players.

There is no better way to attract the young to sport than through having fun . . . and to think it all started with a couple of bunnies happily hopping about Mill Hill village early one summer . . . but more of that later!

BUNBURY TAILS

ZZZZZZ
OLD BILL SAWED AWAY AT A SPECIAL BRANCH
IT'S WICKED.!!
NO BALL TAMPERING..!
VIV, IS THAT BIG ENOUGH..?
NO, SWEAT MAN
THE BUNNY GIRLS KNITTED THE SWEATERS

MIKE ATHERBUN DISCUSSED TACTICS
TRY YOUR LONG HOP!
IAN BUNTHAM BOWLED LIKE THE WIND
ALEC RABBITSTEW TOOK GUARD
GOLDENHARE GOWER SHOWED GRACE
GRAHAM HICKORY SURVEYED THE FIELD

CAUGHT IN THE SLIPS
NEIL HAREBROTHER
-SHORT LEG-
ALLAN RAM CATCHES
SILLY MID OFF
DENNIS LETTUCE
CATCHES WIN MATCHES
RODNEY MUNCH
LITTLE RAJBUN FROM BUNGALORE

NOW WE'RE READY!
BUNBURY C.C. – A PHOTO FINISH TO A HAPPY DAY
LET'S PLAY OUR FIRST GAME NEXT SATURDAY NIGHT
WHEN SATURDAY NIGHT CAME THE MOON BEAMED BRIGHTLY...

...THERE SEEMS TO BE SOMETHING MISSING...!
..WE HAVE NO HOP-POSITION!
HA! HA! HA!

WHO'S THAT LAUGHING...?! WHAT'S YOUR NAME?
GEOFF BOYCAT!
GO HOME AND GET YOUR OWN TEAM TOGETHER!
...SO OFF WENT THE TWO PEEPING TOMS TO NEARBY WHISKERTOWN

CONTINUED ON PAGE 40

The Road to WEM

How did they do it? Captain David English explains how it all began . . .

When Eric Clapton first asked me to captain his cricket XI, from that point onwards I knew that the game could never be quite the same again.

For the first match I took the team back to Ripley, scene of Eric's childhood. As I ran in to bowl I was confronted by Bill Wyman puffing on a fag at short leg, EC and Phil Collins having a chat in the slips (both wearing raincoats as it was chucking it down), and Gary Mason roaring with laughter behind the stumps. I stopped in my tracks to survey the rest of the team. David Essex was charming his fan club at long on. Dennis Waterman was sipping champagne outside the sponsor's tent, and Johnny Keeble was chasing every ball like a terrier. That day, 4000 people stood watching the game in the rain and thousands of pounds were raised for Leukaemia Research.

Champions! David English receives the Crickethon Trophy from Group Captain Leonard Cheshire at Wembley.

For the next four years, the Eric Clapton XI toured the country enthralling crowds with their off-beat style. Our summers were filled with action-packed drama. There was a game against Northants when Allan Border and his lads, after a hard match, stayed to play with us. Dan Essex, aged 11, bowled in tandem with Dennis Lillee. Dennis Waterman, the lone fielder on the leg side, covered every blade of grass as Waugh and Jones smashed the ball to all parts of the field. And finally, Nick Cook took the greatest catch ever seen on the County ground.

The team then adopted the Bunbury mantle when Eric Clapton's work commitments took him abroad. And so, in 1990, the Eric Clapton XI became the Bunbury All Stars. A change of name, but still the same driving compulsion to make as much money for charity through entertaining the crowd, while still having a bit of fun ourselves.

B L E Y

In 1990, the world's best players turned out for the Bunburys: Michael Holding, Dennis Lillee, Allan Border, Dean Jones . . . not bad men to bolster our team of loonies. Gary Lineker played for us against 'Gunner' Goulds' XI at Finchley, where he scored 112 – and a further two goals for Tottenham versus West Ham on the same day. We played for the Prime Minister and Mrs Major at Alconbury where Imran Khan bowled to Azharrudin, the Indian Captain. We fielded against Hampshire when Robin Smith cracked a century in 31 minutes and Paul Terry chipped in with a ton at the other end.

There have been countless heroic efforts to play for the team. Dean Saunders played on June 15 1991, the day he signed for Liverpool for £2.9 million. Ex-New Zealand skipper Geoff Howarth, and Dave Thomas, came out of retirement to play – extremely well – at a moment's notice. Gary Lineker trained all morning with Spurs before catching the 2 o'clock train from Waterloo, to arrive at the ground at 4 o'clock. He then made 59 runs and picked up the 'Man of the Match' award – even with sore limbs and an arm aching from signing a million autographs. Both Andy Sinton, and Simon Barker of QPR, have played in all the games with skill, humour and a great spirit.

However, Eric Clapton's love of the game took a sudden dive at the Beaconsfield game in June 1992. *'Whatever you do,'* said Roger Forrester, his manager, *'look after his hands. He's got a tour of Japan in September, so if he breaks any fingers he won't be able to play.'* The manager's words ticked over in Eric's mind as he stood in the gully. The sun beat down and the cows in the neighbouring field chewed lazily on the cud. It was an idyllic summer's day . . . Gary Mason ran up to bowl, the team's opener smashed it and Eric took off on a valiant dive to catch it, and crunch – his middle finger was shattered. After

deep concern and sympathy from his team-mates, our leader sadly trooped off the field. *'Good luck lads,'* were his parting words. But before he could reach the pavilion, a wasp stung him on his other hand! Eric watched the rest of the game with both his hands immersed in ice buckets. The very next ball was a bouncer that missed the batsman before striking Roger on his head sending the ball spiralling 70 yards towards the boundary. *'Catch it!'* cried Dennis Waterman, the eternal optimist. Ironically, the cricket ground was called *Hit or Miss*. Eric and Roger had certainly been hit and for the rest of the season were sadly missed.

Ten hard victories and the support of our sponsor, EMP, finally took us to Mecca on September 29 1992. We had finally made it! As the rain slanted down, the name of EMP Bunbury reverberated between the twin towers. Long, white flannels replaced the red football strips of Manchester United and Arsenal as the Bunburys became the first cricket team ever to play at Wembley.

The conditions were appalling. In driving rain I paddled out to the wicket to open the innings. Neil Lenham of Sussex delivered a snorter that reared out of a puddle to take off my stump – a hysterical wicket on a historical day.

English and Morris – howzat for openers?

When our opponents, Gary Mason's XI, went in to bat, Joe 'The Hat' Cuby of EMP weaved his magic with his spiralling spinners. Mark Nicholas stood at cover, sweater pulled over his head, while Dennis Waterman patrolled the outfield.

Earlier, Johnny Morris had peppered the stands with well-timed pulls and drives. So had Chris Board and Roland Butcher, crashing the ball into the stands. Joel Garner had leapt into action, ripping the ball off the matting before retiring to the boundary to sign autographs for the fans in the pouring rain.

Rory Bremner ran around enthusiastically, commentating in a thousand voices which, as ever, kept everybody in hysterics. Gary Headley kept wicket chirpily, while Errol Brown bowled with style. Dickie Bird looked on incredulously and I, as captain of this extraordinary outfit, watched what was happening in complete wonder.

The Bunburys amassed 202 in 20 overs, beating Gary Mason's XI by 72 runs. At the end of the game I had the privilege of leading my jubilant team up the famous Wembley steps to receive the Crickethon Trophy from Group Captain Leonard Cheshire. All proceeds from that jubilant day went to the Leonard Cheshire Homes.

Ready for a lap of honour ...

All the boys got drenched in the name of charity and fun. We adjourned to the bar to discuss our exploits, wring out our clothes, and wonder if anyone in the future would remember those mad fools who played in Wembley's first ever cricket match.

Since winning our Wembley Cup Final, the transfer market has gone crazy. Viv Richards, David Gower, John Altman, Ian Botham, Chris Turner, Tony Meo, Paul Davis, Mike Gatting, Barry Gibb, Arthur Cooke, Mike Whitney and the incredible Derek Randall have all joined the team and taken on the famous Bunbury spirit.

THE CAPTAIN'S HALL OF FAME

DAVID ENGLISH

Captain

Former president of RSO Records, David English is author of the bestselling *Bunbury Tails* and a well-known film star to boot. He spoke two lines in *A Bridge Too Far*, one to Robert Redford, the other to Sean Connery, before spending the rest of the film as a dead German. This performance is rumoured to have earned Sir Dickie his Knighthood. David English is Club Captain of Finchley CC and has played for MCC, Middlesex XIs and the Cross Arrows at Lords. This, plus being Ian Botham's side-kick for the last 20 years, well qualifies him to Captain a cricket XI whose general performance can only be described as unruly and occasionally psychopathic.

BILL WYMAN

The legendary ex-Rolling Stones bass player, restaurateur and metal detector still looking for the Holy Grail, Bill has such a stylish left-hand bat he confuses the other side by switching to his right hand when bowling his spinners. He also amazes all by the fags he can get through in his favourite gully position. A pure lover of the game, Bill admits to the cricketing influences of David Gower and Norman Wisdom.

ERIC CLAPTON

A founder member of the EC and Bunbury XIs, Eric is not only the world's premier Rock and Blues guitarist, but the only man to have bowled four wides underarm to Graeme Hick on the Worcester County Cricket Ground. He became interested in horse racing as an owner and a punter, before getting into cricket. In 1984 he asked me if we could go to Lords and watch England play. We arrived at the pavilion but couldn't enter as EC wasn't wearing a tie. I phoned Ian Botham in the dressing room. Soon he was at the door, gave Eric his tie and from that day their mutual love for cricket was forged.

GARY MASON

The most popular heavyweight cricket champion of all time, Gary has a laugh which is even more shattering than his right cross. Gary started boxing in amateur clubs. In 1983 he went to New York and, after sparring with Tyson, was told to take his boxing seriously. It was only after 35 wins that he was beaten by Lennox Lewis, the European champion. Sadly, Gary suffered a bad eye injury that retired him briefly. He then tried, amongst others, Rugby League and commentary, before boxing again. So when Gary wants to bowl, bat and laugh all at once for the Bunburys, nobody argues!

GARY LINEKER

Gary is a true sportsman. He made a total of 194 League appearances for Leicester City before joining Everton in July 1985. Scoring 40 goals in one season, he was then voted Footballer of the Year. After his £2.75m transfer to Barcelona, Gary won a Spanish Cup Winners' Medal in 1988 and the Cup Winners' Cup the following year. He then made a £1.2m move to Tottenham, to become the First Division's Top Scorer of 1991 with 26 goals. The glory continued with a hat trick for England v Poland in the 1986 World Cup Finals, and four goals in the 1990 World Cup. To cap his career in England, Gary won an FA Cup Winner's medal before playing in Japan. He now travels from the 'Land of the Rising Sun' to star for the Bunburys.

IAN BOTHAM

Botham converted the simple bravado and dreams of a village cricketer into epics all over the world. He caught the imagination in a way no other cricketer, past or present, could match. My personal appraisal of his Lordship is too colourful to print in this book, but I can tell you that in 20 years of adventures I have suffered. I have endured: lost nights in pubs; solitary confinement in fishing boats from Stornoway to the Dee; trips to rugby games that have become five-day skirmishes in Irish bars . . . the torture just goes on . . .

WALTER SWINBURN

For a man who only weighs 8st 6lb, Wally can certainly hammer the ball a long way. As a jockey his best season was 1984, with 99 wins. He has won two Derbys – in 1981 on the ill-fated *Shergar* and in 1986 on *Shahrastani*. Wally has won the Oaks, 1000 Guineas twice, Irish Oaks, Irish Derby twice, and many races throughout the world including the 1983 Prix de l'Arc de Triomphe on *All Along*. A great charmer and modern-day D'Artagnan, who will think nothing of riding a hard race in France before flying home to play for his Bunbury pals somewhere in England.

DENNIS WATERMAN

A key player in the Bunbury squad and a founder member of the Clapton XIs, his devastating fielding and damaging bowling are famous. Dennis has starred in many stage and TV roles and, of course as Terry ('leave it out Arfur') in *Minder*. 'Chalkey' is a fanatical footballer and an all-round fun cricketer, who mostly enjoys fielding next to the sponsors' tent for a quick beaker in between overs.

FRAZER HINES

Frazer makes an incredible amount of noise when galloping in from his 40 yard run up to the commentary position – where he'll give you 30 minutes' hilarious barrage. Irrepressible is how best to describe Frazer, whose other obsession is horses. He owns a racehorse and holds a jockey licence, racing regularly in the flat season as an amateur around the British tracks. Hines and Swinburn, a win double? How the mind boggles! Although he's famous as Joe Sugden in *Emmerdale,* Frazer has many film credits to his name. Nearly every year, he appears in pantomime – giving him perfect credentials for a major role in the Bunbury XI.

RORY BREMNER

Rory Bremner is now established as one of Britain's best impressionists, with a reputation for accurate mimicry and topical satire. His award-winning repertoire now extends to over 90 characters, ranging from film actors to television presenters, from comedians to sports commentators, and from politicians to Roy Hattersley. A very fine leg-spin bowler and aggressive batsman, Rory's perpetual banter propels the team throughout the season on a continuous wave of mirth. He continually unsettles the opposing batsmen with a non-stop repertoire of mimicry, aided and abetted by his famous sidekick Andy Peebles.

PETER SCUDAMORE MBE

To supplement his passion for cricket, Peter turned to horse racing to keep his cricketing ambitions alive. But even after riding his first winner in 1979, the cricket still continued. Peter played several times at Arundel in the racing stables competition, where Colin Cowdrey described his bowling technique as *'interesting little tweakers'*. Between fielding like a demon on the same pitch as Michael Holding and opening the batting stylishly for the Bunburys, Peter has become the most successful National Hunt jockey in the history of the sport, managing to win the Championship a magnificent six times.

MIKE READ

Mike's first job was as a vocalist and guitarist in Manchester clubs before working in commercial radio. He joined Radio 1 in 1978, presenting *The Breakfast Show* for five years before hosting Radio 1's weekly singles and album reviews programme, *Roundtable*. He now presents his own radio programme on Capital Gold. His television work includes *Top of the Pops*, *Pop Quiz* and *Saturday Superstore*. Four times *Smash Hits* DJ of the Year, three times *Sun* DJ of the Year and twice Sony DJ of the Year, Mike is a brilliant all-rounder. On the field, his talents vary from accurate bowling to steady batting and we are delighted to have him in the squad.

DEAN SAUNDERS

Born in Swansea, Dean signed for his hometown club as an apprentice. He went to Brighton, Oxford United, Derby and Liverpool, where he won an FA Cup Winner's medal, before signing for Aston Villa in 1992. He won a Coca-Cola Cup Winner's medal this year and has scored over 100 league goals for his club, and played for Wales over 30 times. Another natural cricketer, Dean hits the ball for miles, and hurls himself about the field in all directions. After attacking John Emburey's bowling at Aylesbury, the great off-spinner was seen to roll his eyes and utter, *'hell . . . he's a bit tasty!'* Apparently, a Middlesex contract was offered to Dean the next day.

SIMON BARKER

Simon made around 200 appearances for Blackburn Rovers before he joined Queens Park Rangers. He scored a famous goal against Liverpool in a live television showing of an FA Cup quarter final two years ago and he has played for the England Under-21 team on four occasions. A first class all-rounder, Simon lights up the field wherever he plays. In fact, the combination of Barker, Sinton and Lineker provides an electric network throughout the team.

JOE CUBY

Joe, 'the Hat' Cuby is clearly the most prolific spin bowler in world cricket. He likes to give the 'air a bit of ball' (50 yards in fact), resulting in the ball descending with icicles onto the poor unsuspecting batsman. As chairman of EMP plc, Joe is our sponsor and also our inspiration.

NEAL FOULDS

After becoming a snooker professional in 1983, this former world number three is back to his best form. He won the 1986 BCE International Award and the 1988 Dubai Duty-Free Masters where he defeated Steve Davis. He reached the last four of the 1991 Mercantile Credit, eventually going out 6-4 to Stephen Hendry and beat Steve Davis in the semi-finals of the Benson and Hedges Cup. A real cricket enthusiast who takes his game seriously, Neal is modest about his penetrating bowling and sound batting. Silent but deadly!

ANDY SINTON

Andy joined Queens Park Rangers from Brentford in 1989 and has played for England at schoolboy and adult levels. This smashing Geordie lad began his league career with Cambridge before moving to Brentford in 1985. His excellent midfield work for QPR earned him his first full cap against Poland in the European Championships in November 1991. He has also represented the Football League. His dazzling performances this year for Sheffield Wednesday have helped jettison the team up the Premier Division. As a cricketer, the same quickness of foot and eye make him an outstanding player and a Bunbury star.

JOHNNY *'Legside Stumper'* KEEBLE

An incredible athlete who cheerfully travels thousands of miles every year playing the game and supporting charity. Like all wicket keepers, goalies and drummers, John throws himself into everything.
He says:
'12 years of success with Spandau Ballet has not diminished my cricketing desires . . . I have had the pleasure of befriending and playing with many of my heroes in a myriad of charity games, benefit matches and very wet games. No game is too far, no pitch too muddy for this team!'

RISING STARS

If ever there was a boy destined to take the field for England it was Liam Botham. As a valued member of the English Schools Cricket Association (ESCA) and with his natural cricketing skills, he is edging towards a future at Test level – and he's not the only one.

Botham Jnr, a strapping six-footer competed in the historic ESCA U-15s match in 1992, with the rest of a lively England team, against a determined South African side. Liam, who is 17 this summer, is a very important member of an England side bursting with talent.

The future bodes well for the development of our fledgling internationals and the evidence is there on the field. Liam is the perfect all-rounder, just the Lionheart England needs. He is also supported by stylish young batsmen in the shape of Philip Ayres and Tom Newman.

Liam Botham

Credit must be given to the organization skills of ESCA. The celebrity cricket matches, played as many as 20 times a year, help raise the profile of the England youth team. The maverick band of musical legends and sporting heroes all take part because of their love of the game. All monies raised go towards national charities, and the U-15s – the *Young Bunburys*, as they are affectionately known, benefit as well. And what a safe commodity they are investing in.

David Sales is an awesome young batsman. The Surrey CC player won the Daily Telegraph National Batting Award and scooped the Sir Jack Hobbs Trophy as the most outstanding U-16 English cricketer of 1993. Lancashire CC player Andrew Flintoff scored an impressive century against the Orange State Invitation X1 at Bloemfontein on the U-15s tour of South Africa. The 100 was all the more impressive because it was hit off just 105 balls. He smacked the boundaries 16 times and recorded a huge six. Daniel Kirkland took the award for best bowler at the last Bunbury Festival in 1992, and intends to snatch it again. Mark Snell also returns for the *Young Bunburys*, after a successful tour with the team in South Africa, and plays at his second Festival. Wicket-keeper David Nash is also handy with a cricket bat. The Middlesex player fired his interest in cricket by watching Test Matches from the age of five.

England U-15s manager Derek Day summed up the pride felt for this youth team when he said:

'It is a privilege to manage a national side that conducts itself with decorum on and off the field. They fight to the bitter end when all seems lost, they play hard at all times keeping within the laws of the game and with the spirit that the game should be played with.'

Teamwork is essential for the U-15s to succeed. ESCA gives them opportunities to play together regularly and to develop cohesive styles. Defenders complement attackers and good fielders assist penetrative bowlers. Getting the ball back accurately and speedily assists the whole team. Sharp concentration and quick reactions are the qualities that spread admiration and affection throughout the team. Telepathy helps, but a firm understanding and clear thinking will do. Powerful, confident openers need to be assured that their respective partners are on the same wavelength. No suicide runs for this team.

Morale and character are extremely important for England players and every team needs personalities on its side. Enter Liam Botham, lion-cub of a player. Yorkshire-born Liam attends Rossall School in Fleetwood and has competed in sports there, and has played rugby for Lancashire. But it's his performances at the crease that matter most to cricket's desperadoes. Die-hard England fans can see that the signs are good.

The strong-arm bowl and the boisterous appeal are all familiar if still to be perfected. He can slug them as high as his Dad and shows the recklessness that will make him an unpredictable and exciting player. But he is obviously an individual with an independent streak. He is on the books at Hampshire CCC and is happy to forge his career with a southern county despite his northern roots. Gregarious and social, he breaks through barriers, and forges friendships at all matches, very much a team player. Just be grateful he didn't choose rugby . . .

'Although I had a pretty good cricket career at school, I did not make the final side. But that should prove to any other lad who is disappointed, that it is not the end of the world.'

Ian Botham

photo left – Like father, like son? Source: The Daily Telegraph

SPOT THE

DIFFERENCE

There are 10 differences.
Can you spot them all?

DOWN UNDER

'Welcome to the conquerors of Bunnybados,' shone the neon lights above the Odeon Leicester Hare.

The victorious Bunburys were attending a film show in their honour hosted by the TCCB (Take Care Cuddle a Bunny).

'Over here for a picture!' shouted photographer Patrick Twitchfield.

'They want to show us some newsreel or other,' said Goldenhare.

> KAPIL DOVE'S TEAM HIT FOR SIX BY THE AUSSIE BATTING CAVALIERS.
> NATION'S CRICKET LOVERS ENTHRALLED BY DARING DINGOS AND CANNY KOALAS.

The message was clear for all to see emblazoned on the screen.

'What do you think of that bunch?' whispered Buntham to Old Holbun.

There was no reply. The manager's seat was empty.

'He's gone,' said Pooch, *'and just left this note.'*

Buntham read the note in the half-light of the cinema. *'Enjoy yourselves tonight. Report to the club tomorrow morning at nine o'clock. The challenge is on Down Under!'*

'Brisbun and Melbun seem a long way away,' said Allan Ram, the following morning.

'Are we flying British Hareways from Buck-teeth Row?'

'No, no. I have a little surprise for you. Come this way,' laughed Old Holbun. *'Give me a hand, lads, to open these garage doors. Let me introduce you to the amazing Bunnymobile.'*

Spellbound, the bunnies gazed at the bright shining machine.

'What is this, Old Holbun?' piped up Rajbun.

'Well chaps, while you were away a couple of friends of mine, Nigel Bunsell and Merling Stoss, came up with the design and Greasebun, our mechanic, knocked it up to my specifications. It's amphibious and, by jove, it can fly! Rod and Denno, you know the way, so you can navigate. Climb aboard everyone. Next stop Brisbun!'

'At the Gabba Ground here in Brisbun there have been some hare-raising batting by the Aussies, but Allan Bounder is on 94 not out,' commentator Richie Bunaud's voice crackled through the loudspeaker.

The shirt-sleeved crowd roared its appreciation in reply.

'Phew! Just look at that lot,' sighed Goldenhare Gower.

High up in the stands there were koalas, wallabies, dingos, crocodiles, lizards, emus, wombats and even the odd platypus.

Buntham prepared to bowl.

'Go home, Beefy! You've got no chance,' cried one of the lizards, with a whippish tongue.

'I'll give you fair dinkum, mate,' mumbled Buntham, starting his run.

Buntham charged in, but Bounder was fully prepared. CRASH! The ball went into the crowd, landing straight into the pouch of a dozing kangaroo. With a sudden start the kangaroo came back to life and hopped off into the distance at a furious pace.

'After him,' yelled Buntham. *'Come back you Wally!'*

Along the streets of Brisbun ran the Bunburys in pursuit of the woolly jumper.

'Faster!' Buntham urged.

'Faster? Who do you think I am . . . Sebastian Doe? panted Allan Ram.

'We'll never catch him,' shouted Goldenhare. *'Get me the Batmobile, Robin.'*

'Don't you mean the Bunnymobile, skipper?' corrected Jackrabbit.

'What? Oh, yes . . . sorry old chap. It must be the sun!'

Into the orange-red desert the kangaroo leapt on pursued by the hot, cross bunnies. They drove through tumbleweed towns and past watering holes. Finally, there was no more water – just the wilderness of the bush.

Putt, putt, putt . . . the Bunnymobile came to a halt.

'Well, that's blown it,' said Thumpage. *'We've ran out of luck and water!'*

Parched and weary, the Bunburys continued on foot across the shimmering sand. They nearly melted in the heat.

'What's that?' Asked Whiskers, straining his eyes. *'Is it a mirage?'*

Together the bunnies peered into the distance. Slowly the blurred image became clearer.

'I must be seeing things,' said Viv Radish.

'G'day! Welcome to Hare's Rock. My name's Dingo Den. I'm a bush photographer. This is my assistant, Alice Springs.'

'How do, boys. You look pooped. You think this is bad? I come from Melbun where the crows fly backwards to keep the dust out of their eyes,' said Alice.

'You haven't seen a kangaroo come through here with a cricket ball in his pouch?' enquired John Emberbunny.

'Pull the other one, mate. It plays "Waltzing Mathilda"!' roared the doubting dingo.

Dingo Den and Alice Springs listened thoughtfully as the Bunburys told them of their plight.

'OK, I believe you,' said Den at last. *'You'd better come with us. Nobody will find you down here.'*

The bunnies were taken to the pinnacle of Hare's Rock. The view was breathtaking.

Back at the Gabba Ground there was pandemonium. In the middle, Allan Bounder and Grog Matthews were still running.

'One hundred and one, one hundred and two,' panted the Aussie skipper.

'Still no sign of the ball and those Poms, Sir Don,' reported Ray Bite.

'Right! The search is on,' announced the Aussie chairman. *'Alert the cats in Purrth and the dingos on the Great Terrier Reef. We've got to find those Bunburys.'*

'Now, Denno, you've got the strongest arm. Bring your boomerangs to me,' said Sir Don.

Climbing onto the pavilion roof, Lettuce summoned up all his strength and hurled the boomerangs towards the outback.

At Hare's Rock the Bunburys were waiting anxiously.

'I feel so giddy,' mumbled Rajbun. *'My head is going round in circles.'*

The first wave of Lettuce's boomerangs caught the bunnies on the hop. Glinting in the sun, they passed overhead.

'Are they UFOs?' cried Pooch.

'No! No! What do they say?' said Ram, reading the underside of the boomerangs. *'Bunburys where are you?'*

By now the boomerangs had disappeared.

'Quick, Goldenhare, get the team together,' ordered Old Holbun.

Standing on each other's backs, the Bunburys formed a bunny pyramid, with Rajbun perched right on top. Patiently the precarious group waited on the massive rock.

'Here they come again, Raj. Now stretch!' cried Buntham.

Rajbun reached up as the boomerangs whooshed overhead, but failed to make contact. Then with one big effort, Buntham used his enormous power and pushed.

Fingers fully extended, Rajbun caught the last boomerang, which took him whirling back to Brisbun.

Together the Bunburys stood and watched their little friend fly off into the red sun, with his turban unravelling behind him.

When Rajbun fell into the arms of Dennis Lettuce, he caught the fast bowler in a spin.

'Well taken, Denno!' screamed the crowd. *'First catch today.'*

'You must come quickly and rescue my pals,' Rajbun told the baffled Aussies. *'Right lads . . . get out the Flying Doctor,'* ordered Sir Don Bradbun. *'Raj, you show the way.'*

Carefully following the turban's trail, Sir Don and his players were able to find the Bunburys. What a reunion!

'It's good to see you again,' said the relieved bunnies, embracing their rivals.

'Have you got any refreshments?' asked the hungry bunnies.

'Yeah, how about a picnic at hanging rock?' said Dingo Den.

'I suppose we'll have to abandon the match,' pondered Old Holbun.

'You've got to be joking, mate,' replied Sir Don. *'When I left, the boys had scored 1000 runs and were still going strong.'*

Just then, a stranger holding a cricket ball joined the gathering.

'Is this what you're looking for?' asked the run-away kangaroo apologetically.

TAILS FROM THE SLIPS

Rock 'n' Bowl

At the Bunbury game at Brentford FC, New Zealand Test star Richard Snell was performing for the opposition. Out onto the pitch strode the openers for the Bunburys, Chris Broad and Bill Wyman.

'Just a quick word, Richard,' I whispered. *'One of them plays for England, the other for the Rolling Stones.'*

To our complete surprise, Snell started to bowl gentle off-breaks to Chris who then proceeded to dispatch them with great gusto out of the stadium with the utmost style and relish.

Meanwhile, the first ball to Bill shaved his midriff, the next took his 'Benson and Hedges' out of his pursed lips, the third was a 'sandshoe crusher' and the fourth shattered the hopping Billy's wicket.

As an amazed Bill sadly trouped off to the pavilion, the embarrassed fast bowler admitted, *'Cripes, I got them round the wrong way!'* Chris Broad, a Rolling Stone? Better get Mick on the phone . . .

Bill Wyman – rolled out!

Antigua Blues

After a game at Finchley, the incredible Stan Webb's R and B band were playing in a nearby marquee. Unbeknown to Eric Clapton, I had arranged for his guitar to be brought along, just in case the musical mood took him. *'Come on Eric, it would be a tremendous end to a great Bunbury day'*, I pleaded.

Back in the bar, the banter was thick and furious. Suddenly the unmistakable chords of *Layla* could be heard clearly above the noisy din. I had never seen a bar empty so quickly. There in the tent, Eric the maestro was strutting his stuff with the blues band.

For three hours, 500 enthralled people jogged to the music.

'Marvellous,' said Eric, as a horizontal reveller sped past his nose. *'Reminds me of the good old days.'*

For the next three years, Eric's appearance after the fixture became an event. Blues circles from Chicago to Chingford wondered why the maestro would want to perform in a London beer tent. There were even bootleg tapes made – *Eric Clapton Live with the Bunburys at Finchley.*

Then, in the fourth year, Eric phoned. *'Arfur'*, he said (he always calls me Arfur), *'I've got to call it a day.'* He then went off to Antigua for a well-deserved rest.

But it was too late. Whilst sunbathing, he overheard Brian Johnston on the BBC World Service. *'Don't forget to go to Finchley where the Bunburys will be performing, followed by the usual wonderful performance by Eric Clapton.'*

The usually cool Eric was then seen hurling a stranger's radio far out into the Caribbean, crying, *'That blasted English, I'll kill 'im!'*

Eric Clapton – Layla'd low in Antigua.

The Last Post

We had arranged an early season warm-up game at Finchley against the Acton and District Royal Mail Sorting Office,Third XI. That weekend, Ian Botham and Viv Richards were staying with me. *'Do you fancy coming up to Finchley and watching a bit of cricket?'* I enquired. *'Yeah, no problem, Dave'*, replied the two legends. *'We could do with an afternoon off'*.

When we arrived at the cricket pavilion I met the opposing skipper, a large beaming Jamaican. *'Hey man, I got de dilemma,'* he groaned. *'Two of me men have not turned up.' 'Listen Leroy,'* I said. *'I might be able to help you. I met these two blokes in a pub, who reckon they can play a bit. Why not give them a game?'* Leroy wasn't too impressed. *'Well, I suppose it's better than playing with only nine men,'* he mumbled.

I nipped outside and summoned Ian and Viv. When the two stars stood silhouetted in the door of the pavilion, there was an eerie silence of disbelief, followed by a crash as Leroy's pint of shandy dropped from his hand. *'Here they are Leroy, apparently this one bowls a bit and this fellow reckons he can bat.' 'What?'* blurted Leroy. *'Where do we get changed, skipper?'* enquired Ian and Viv politely.

That afternoon, Botham and Richards carved up the Bunbury attack, peppering the roofs of North Finchley. Ian and Viv are now honorary members of the Acton Post Office.

THE GOOD GUYS

These are the cricketing bunnies from Bunbury village who travel the world to pitch their skills against devious opponents

Early one day, Jan Brychta and I were sitting by a cricket ground at Mill Hill village in North London, chatting away and dreaming as usual. Suddenly, up jumped a couple of rabbits who ran across the pitch. *'Look Jan,'* I said, as an idea evolved. *'The frisky one could be Ian Buntham and the other quieter one could be Goldenhare Gower. Viv Radish would be a bunny opponent from sunny Bunnybados; Dennis Lettuce would have burrowed up from Down Under – he would play at Melbun or Brisbun or even at Hares Rock against Allan Bounder and the dogs from The Great Terrier Reef; Little Rajbun would come from Bungalore and be the team's mascot . . . what do you think?'* My mind was racing as mentally I was creating more and more bunny characters whose names and personalities linked perfectly with the most well-known cricketing legends of today.

There was no immediate reply from the great Czech. His imagination had also been caught and he was busy sketching away. Before our eyes the characters started to emerge on his pad. As usual he had managed to capture them exactly as I had seen them in my mind's eye.

GREASEBUN

He's the Bunbury's baseballin', slam dunking, jive talkin', hip hoppin', streetwise, mechanic and general handydude. But don't let this wisecracker from the Bronx fool you. He's a straightforward mechanical genius with a master's degree in engineering.

Greasebun may not be a world-class player, but he can turn his hand to any game. It's his inventive skill that gets the Bunburys out of many a tight spot. Greasebun can make an engine out of kitchen sinks, baked bean tins, rubber bands and even smoked kippers . . .

MIKE ATHERBUN

Tipped to be the next captain of the Bunburys, Mike has a laid-back style, he's into yoga and transcendental meditation and spends most of his time in bed. This is why he manages to stay cool while everyone else is flapping!

When not playing cricket, he's climbing up a rock face 500 feet in the air, blindfolded, and with one hand tied behind his back. He reckons it helps to focus his mental concentration. His sporting skills, plus the ability to scale any mountain or building, makes him a particular asset to the team.

IAN BUNTHAM

He is the hero, swashbuckler, rebel and 'fight the good fight' member of the team. Boisterous, rumbustious, mischievous, a practical joker, a rabbit for any crisis, a lover of good causes and an extrovert with a heart the size of Bunbury Green. He likes to get his own way and feels that he is always right.

He is light on his feet, and is an all-round sportsman who excels at golf, marksmanship and football. A rabbit who is always in the front-line of attack, he even admits to having some 'edited highlights' in his hair.

VIV RADISH

He is immensely proud, extremely laid-back, strong and silent – an introvert who complements Ian Buntham's extrovert nature.

A real wow with the ladies, who love his snappy dressing, elegant ways and charm, he likes to laugh and is loyal and generous. Viv is a 'master blaster' cricketer. A brilliant all-round sportsman and a strong back-up in attack.

OLD HOLBUN AND MARY

Holbun is the team's guru who always has the right answers. He is very wise and has an endless supply of stories to tell. Mary is a great enthusiast of the Bunburys and really supports the white-whiskered Holbun, and he in turn adores her. Together, they are the touchstone for the health and happiness of the entire team.

As firm Bunburys' supporters, Holbun's only athleticism is the mental agility of his storytelling, Mary's is the resilience to oversee the needs of a maverick team.

RAJBUN FROM BUNGALORE

Rajbun saw an article in the *Delhi Mail* one day about the Bunburys of England. He packed his bags and came to join his heroes, and he is now the team mascot. He is so keen to be a Bunbury he has endeared himself to the senior players, particularly Buntham, who protects him. Naive in worldly ways, but cute in ideas on how to win games, his determination to do well has made him a a firm favourite with them all.

Bungalore and Bunbury are twin towns.

GOLDENHARE GOWER

Goldenhare has a persona of effortless charm – he is vague, kind, wise, and never gets unruffled. A real gentleman who could easily pass as a Noel Coward personality. He's a good dancer, smooth talker, and manipulator.

Slim, graceful and a natural-born athlete, Goldenhare Gower is the most gifted cricketer of them all. His tight curly blond hair is his trademark.

RODNEY MUNCH & DENNIS LETTUCE – *Double Trouble*

Both are rough and ready rascals who are full of mischief and a little cunning. Fond of carrot juice, they have a boisterous sense of humour and are loyal and reliable.

Lettuce is the greatest, most athletic fast bowler of all time, Munch, *(below),* the great Aussie wicket-keeper who catches everything. Together they are known as 'Double Trouble'.

...CONTINUED FROM PAGE SEVEN

FIRST BUND AID
WHISKERTOWN MADE 176. BUNBURY BATTED SUPERBLY, ATHERBUN AND RABBIT-STEW CHIPPED AWAY AT THE TOTAL. BUNTHAM FOLLOWED, THEN RADISH....
TEN TO WIN AND BUNTHAM HAD RUN OUT OF PARTNERS. SURELY IT HAD TO BE THE END FOR BUNBURY WITH THEIR ELEVENTH MAN OUT FOR THE COUNT. SUDDENLY... THERE TOTTERING ON THE PAVILION STEPS WAS RAJBUN.
OVER HERE RAJ..!!
IN CAME IMRAN. IT WAS A FEARSOME BOUNCER. THE BALL RAPPED RAJBUN'S BAT AND WENT THROUGH THE SLIPS FOR FOUR. BUNBURY HAD WON THE GAME.
AS GEOFF BOYCAT PRESENTED THE FOURTEEN CARROT TROPHY TO BUNTHAM THE BUNBURY SKIPPER SMILED:
WELL DONE RAJ..!
YOU CAN KEEP THIS!
THAT NIGHT, YOUNG RAJBUN SLEPT WITHOUT BATTING AN EYELID. HIS TRUSTY BAT BY HIS SIDE, HE FELL INTO A DEEP DREAM.
TODAY BUNBURY— TOMORROW... LORD'S!

THE TRIUMPHANT BUNBURYS WERE RARING TO GO!
WHO ARE WE PLAYING TODAY?
GRAHAM POOCH AND THE DOGS FROM BARKING C.C.
BUT RAIN STOPPED PLAY. THE PLAYERS MOOCHED AROUND THE DRESSING ROOM.
LET'S WATCH TOP OF THE HOPS..!
LITTLE RAJBUN WAS STARING UP AT THE BATS!
AH! THIS ONE BELONGED TO JACK HOPPS...AND DR. W.G. GRASS...HE SCORED...
...WHY IS THIS CASE EMPTY?
THE EMPTY CASE... LET ME TELL YOU ABOUT EXCALIBAT!
IN THE YEAR 300 B.B. (BEFORE BUNTHAM) KING ARTHUR BARKER AND QUEEN BUNNIVERE RULED OVER THIS LAND FROM CASTLE OF BUNELOT.
ONE DAY BUNBURYE WAS INVADED BY IVAN THE TERRIBULL AND HIS BUNBARIANS.
THE BUNNIES TRIED TO DEFEND THEIR LAND BUT THEY WERE TERRIBULLY OUTNUMBERED
EVERYONE INSIDE?!
THEY RETREATED TO THE SANCTUARY OF THE CASTLE

WHAT CAN WE DO...?
KING ARTHUR CALLED HIS TRUSTY KNIGHTS SIR LAUGHALOT, THE DUKE OF HEAD-IN-BURROW AND ALLAN THE LAMB TO HIS CHAMBER.
SIRE, WHAT OF OLDE HOLBUN THE MAGICIAN...?
CARROT JUICE
OLDE HOLBUN YOU ARE SUMMONED TO THE KING!
THE KING NEEDS YOUR MAGIC, OH WISE ONE.!!
A MIRACLE HE SHALL HAVE!!
OLDE HOLBUN WORKED BY DAY AND BY KNIGHT.
FINALLY HE REVEALED HIS SECRET WEAPON...
MAY I PRESENT EXCALIBAT!?
ONE BY ONE THE NOBLES TRIED TO LIFT THE BAT OUT OF THE STONE BUT NONE OF THEM WAS ABLE TO...
FIND ME THE RABBIT WHO CAN LIFT EXCALIBAT!
OFF WENT THE KNIGHTS IN SHINING ARMOUR...

CONTINUED ON PAGE 72...

TRIVA QUIZ

1 Name the two players who played cricket for England and football for Scotland?

2 Which man wearing a number seven shirt took a record number of corners for England?

3 Name three players whose surnames are named after flowers, and who all once played for Manchester United FC?

4 Which famous cricketer scored three 'ducks' in the same game?

5 Which England players have the nicknames Judge, Cat, Dude and Gus?

6 A famous ex-England cricketer walked over the Alps for a charitable cause – who was he?

7 Which current player has opened the batting for South Africa and Australia?

8 Which test cricketer is called 'Billy the Kid'?

9 In recent times, which two teenager cricketers starred for their country?

10 There are three players with names beginning with G, who have captained England in the last 10 years, who are they?

1. *Geoff Boycott and Denis Law* **2.** *Barry Sheene* **3.** *Denis Violet, Jackie Blanchflower and Ted McDougall(!)* **4.** *Viv Richards. On his debut for Antigua, Viv was given out in the first innings. Being the 'new kid on the block', the fans threatened to burn down the stands. He was quickly reinstated, only to be out for 0 again and with a big 0 in the second innings.* **5.** *Robin Smith, Phil Tufnel, Devon Malcolm and Angus Fraser.* **6.** *Ian Botham.* **7.** *Kepler Wessels* **8.** *Craig McDermott of Australia* **9.** *Sachin Ten Dulkar and Vinod Kambli of India* **10.** *Gatting, Gooch and Gower*

Courtney in the act

Roger who?

Jump to it! The PM consults Smith-Eccles.

Who won Mr.Universe in 1976? Left to right: a. Francis Mughan b. Robert Redford c. David English.
The correct answer is c.

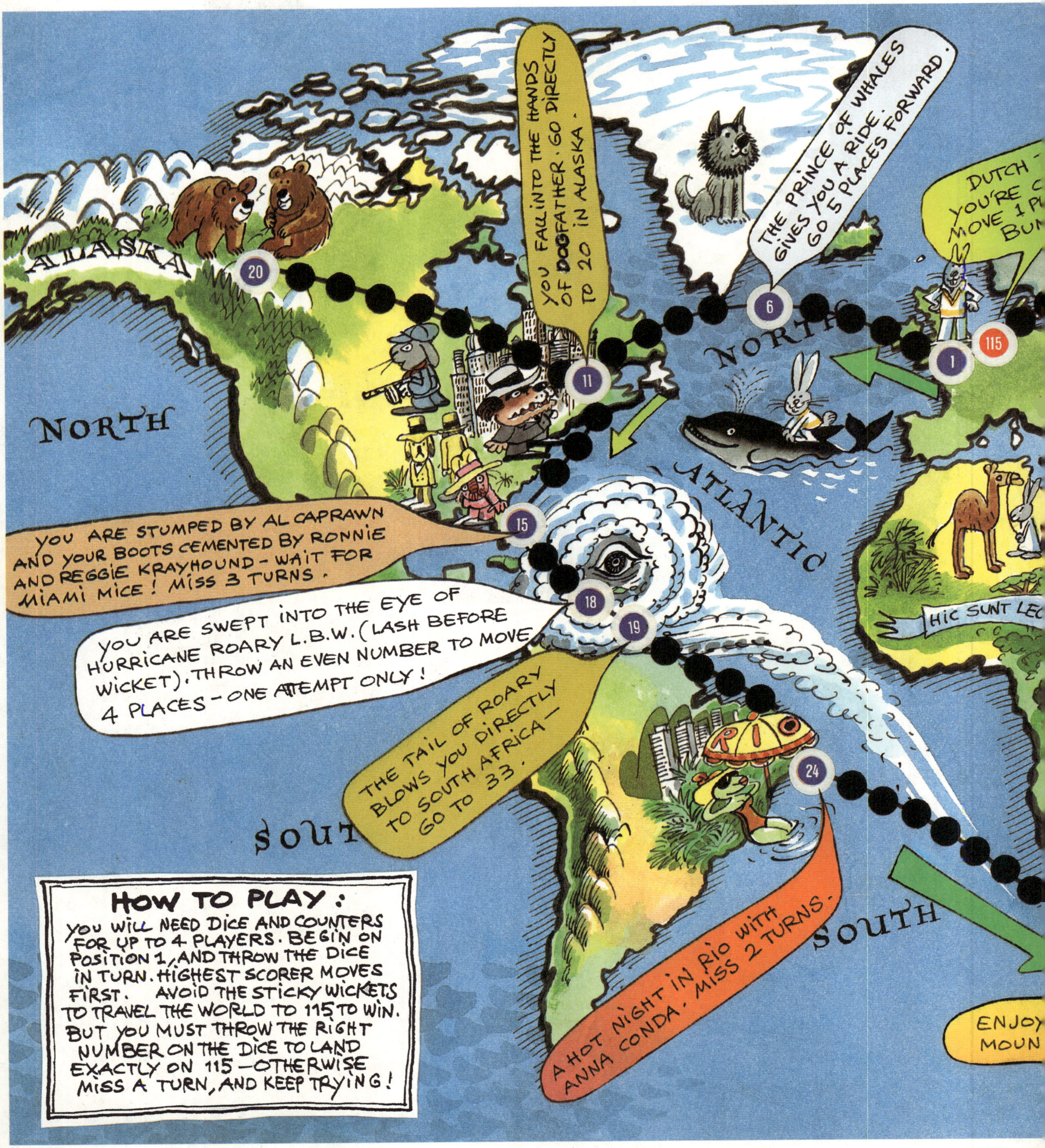

HOW TO PLAY:

YOU WILL NEED DICE AND COUNTERS FOR UP TO 4 PLAYERS. BEGIN ON POSITION 1, AND THROW THE DICE IN TURN. HIGHEST SCORER MOVES FIRST. AVOID THE STICKY WICKETS TO TRAVEL THE WORLD TO 115 TO WIN. BUT YOU MUST THROW THE RIGHT NUMBER ON THE DICE TO LAND EXACTLY ON 115 — OTHERWISE MISS A TURN, AND KEEP TRYING!

GLOBAL INNINGS GAME

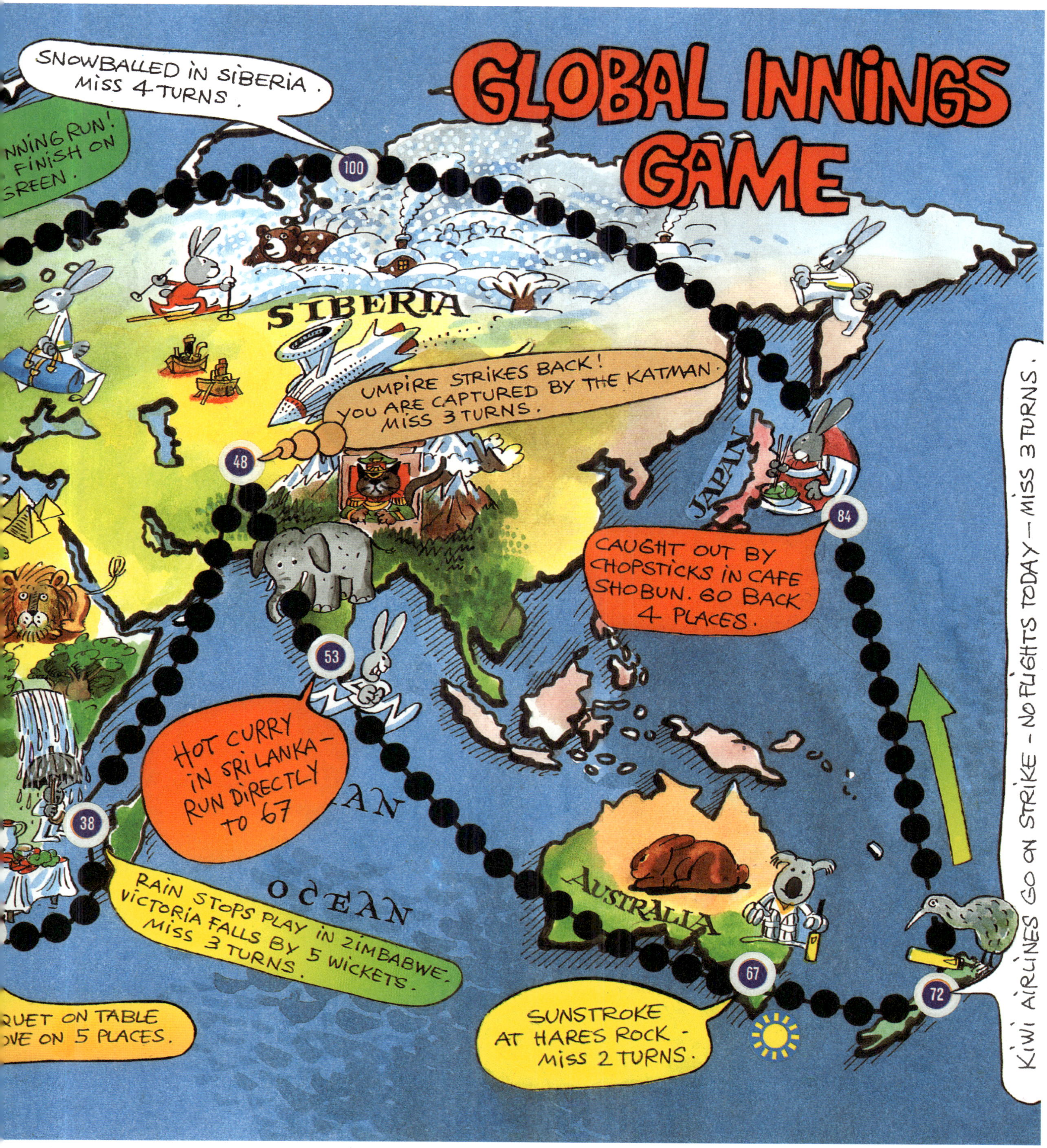

JUNIOR WORLD CUP COMPETITORS

A love for cricket always begins during the school years when there is plenty of time for sport. People ask me why Indian players are great straight drivers, whilst the West Indians are happy hookers. Well, in the back streets of crowded Bombay, the lads prepare the wicket in between parked cars. If the ball is hit over the car, the person is out, so hitting it straight between the cars is the only way to succeed. In the West Indies, cricket is first played on the beach with a hard rubber ball. The players stand on the edge of the ocean waiting for the waves to roll in. As they roll out they bowl to each other on the thin layer of water. This makes the ball leap up, quickening the reflexes and developing a player's hook shot pretty sharpish!

In 1996 the very first Junior World Cup of cricket will take place in this country. Organized by Bunbury and the English Schools Cricket Association. The World Cup will involve 10 competing countries. It will give youngsters around the world their greatest chance to develop more cricketing skill, make friends, be competitive and to enjoy the rivalry and spirit of the game at the highest competitive level. An added bonus will be allowing us to look at the test teams of the next millennium and be able to recognize those youngsters who played in the first ever Junior World Cup.

How the system of schools' cricket is structured varies throughout the 10 competing teams. On the following pages we have tried to give a little insight into how the system works in all the different countries.

AUSTRALIA – *The greatest rivalry in the game*

'Talented cricketers are spotted by State Association Development Officers through trials and games, and the lucky ones are selected for their first national competition'

Last year the Aussies snatched the Ashes away from a hapless England on their own territory and happily strolled back Down Under. Never has cricketing rivalry been as intense as when these two countries play. In fact, most Australian players enjoy, if that's the right word, their cricket most when they are knocking the Pommies for six. But to maintain this fierce rivalry the Australians need to keep producing outstanding young players such as the dazzling bowler Shane Warne.

The emphasis on aspiring young cricketers in Australia has moved away from schools. In fact, the schools system has broken down to the point where it has virtually disappeared from all except the private schools, which rarely produced high-calibre players anyway. They certainly cannot be held responsible for the legendary talents of Allan Border who has notched up over 11,000 runs in Tests.

The real strength lies in district and club cricket. The state associations give considerable resources to junior cricket so that youngsters go from club cricket into district cricket, where the state teams are selected. Each district team has up to five teams, with many of the lower-grade teams being club cricketers of school age. Sir Donald Bradman is the most famous name in Australian cricket and his success at the sport has spread enthusiasm across the vast plains of Australia.

Australia has very strong inter-state competitions, which include under-12s right up to the under-17s. The talented cricketers are spotted by state association development officers through trials and games, and the lucky ones go on to their first national competition for all states and territories in the under-17s and under-19s.

Now if a 12-year-old schoolboy wanted to play for Australia, this is the route he'd take. He might play for the West Pymble team in the under-12s in the Gordon district of Sydney. By 15, he might try out to play in the 5th grade of the Gordon district team while also trying to make the New South Wales team in the under-17s. He would work his way up the grade ladder and try to get into the NSW state representative sides. He might also try to get into the Australian cricket academy and play in the Australian under-19 teams, just like star players Merv Hughes and Dean Jones. England go over to Australia in December to try and win back the prized Ashes and continue the competitive rivalry between the teams.

HOLLAND – *Making up for lost time*

'Holland have won the European Championships at soccer. The face of cricket could change dramatically if they achieve the same sort of success with a bat and ball'

Holland are new to the international cricketing arena, but are nevertheless likely to produce successful teams in the very near future. So big boys – beware!

In The Netherlands, boys and girls become cricketers by learning the game in multi-sport clubs. As the cricket sections of the clubs are all affiliated to football or hockey clubs on the same sports complex, budding cricketers are nearly always footballers or hockey players looking for some sport to play in the summer.

Cricket has never really been popular in Dutch schools, as school sport has never been part of the Dutch culture. The high standard of young soccer and hockey players is down to intensive coaching and excellent organization by sports clubs. Although the same principles apply to cricket, there are only around 5000 cricketers in the country, with only about 1000 who are under 18. This compares with over 1 million active footballers.

Almost all these 1000 young cricketers will have been exposed to professional coaching at some stage, along with training camps, regional and national leagues and national squads at all levels from the age of 12 upwards. The national squads in the three oldest age groups (13–14, 15–16, and 17–18) tour England every season to pit their skills, with considerable success, against the best county teams.

Although the club system has produced three English county players in recent years – Paul-Jan Bakker, Roland Lefevre and Andre van Troost – there is a danger that there is an over-concentration of juniors across the 12 largest clubs. These are the ones with the most resources and currently attract 75 per cent of all the young cricketers in The Netherlands. This is a narrow base from which to supply a national team which has held three ICC trophies (first in 1986, second in 1990 and the third in 1994) and can hold its own with any non-Test playing country.

The National Cricket Association is now making valiant efforts to promote awareness of the game in schools. This is helped by television and, hopefully, by the publicity given to the game by the national team recently qualifying in Kenya for the World Cup. The association will also appoint a professional youth cricket promoter to coordinate this task, and to ensure the broader development of the game.

INDIA – *Producing fine home-grown talent*

'Many young boys watch their heroes Kapil Dev and Anil Kumble play at the Gymkhane Stadium in Bombay and dream of emulating them'

The Gymkhane Stadium in Bombay is the home of Indian cricket. Many young boys watch their heroes Kapil Dev and fellow-bowler Anil Kumble play there and dream of emulating their talent. To do this, however, they must first learn all the skills and subtleties of the absorbing game.

Schools' cricket is still very much the starting ground for all Indian cricket, but it has lost its importance to age-group cricket. There is so much cricket for the under-19s at the inter-state level that it has taken the shine off the old school rivalries as in, say, an Eton-Harrow match.

Players like Tendulkar and Kambli are exceptionally talented cricketers who made the jump to junior state cricket after playing a couple of inter-school matches. Both of them came from the cricket school of a Bombay coach called Achrekar.

India's best cricketers are now found in age-group cricket at the inter-state level, rather than school and university cricket as it used to be in Sunil Gavaskar's time. The cricketing board organizes regular age group coaching camps, throughout the year regionally, and centrally in summer during the vacation.

In the major cities, the private clubs promote well-structured cricket. They seek out the talented young players and take them on. Since many of these clubs are sponsored by companies, they can offer young cricketers a monthly allowance. Young players can also receive scholarships from public companies. They too, all dream of playing at the Eden Gardens in Calcutta or taking on England at the Green Park in Kanpur.

The city league forms the basis of most cricket in India. The state association depends upon the city leagues to pick the best players. Youngsters playing in these leagues stand a better chance of getting through the system. Also the nets and grounds belonging to the state association are better kept. The age-group teams are picked by their performance in inter-school matches, but the talented players are already playing city leagues by the age of 15. They are also not far off joining current team members, such as the outstanding batsman Navjot Sidhu, in the National side.

NEW ZEALAND – *Home of Sir Richard*

'It is to the youngsters that the New Zealand Associations must look, and therefore the future is very much in their hands'

Sir Richard Hadlee was an immortal cricketer. He represented his country in an amazing 86 Tests accumulating a record-making 431 wickets in over 17 years. Unfortunately, New Zealand has not managed to produce another legend since he gracefully retired four years ago. It is to today's youngsters that the Associations must look and the country's cricketing future is very much in their hands.

There is much organization on behalf of cricket in New Zealand schools. The primaries (under-13s) send their teams to the clubs each Saturday morning at 8.30am and they will play until noon. Some clubs have 1000 members or more, when you include the juniors. From these young players, representative teams meet in annual tournaments at Christmas time, with the same regions in the senior provinces.

Girls also mix in at this level, although the rules have only recently been changed to allow them to be represented. In the under-13s a 5oz ball is used, but the older boys change to the heavier men's ball while the women stay with the 5oz. A hard ball is discouraged for the under-10s, with five to seven year-olds playing 'kwik kricket', a condensed version with a plastic bat, ball and set of stumps. The basic cricketing skills are learned here at school, without fear or worry of injury. From secondary school onwards, boys play in their age groups up to the first XI. Only a few jump these stages, and talent scouts are always looking out for skilled players.

Despite being a sparsely populated country, New Zealand can still boast three fantastic grounds: Eden Park in Auckland, Lancaster Park in Christchurch and the Basin Reserve in Wellington.

New Zealand skipper Martin Crowe was discovered playing cricket in primary school games at the Cornwall Club and was taken on as a team member at Auckland Grammar, even before he joined the school, but that was unusual. He had the advantages of an older brother who was already captain of the Grammar XI, a vast reputation as the record scoring primary school batsman, and a zealous father who organized matches and sat on committees!

Girls find few schools willing to organize cricket games for them, but there are representative age-group teams. Emily Drumm is a talented player who captained her female under-16 Auckland Association team and the Secondary School XI.

PAKISTAN – *The thorn in England's side*

'Matches between the leading schools were watched by big crowds and the outstanding performers gained a big reputation, even before they were old enough to start college'

Pakistan has always produced competitive and aggressive players. Batsmen Javed Miandad and Salim Malik are vividly remembered for their cricketing style on their overseas tours, as are the pace bowlers Waquar Younis and Wasim Akram. To produce this high standard of players the schools must have a successful and well-organized cricketing programme.

Cricket in schools at the time of Independence was very well organized. There were certain schools that were known as cricket nurseries and it was from these schools that the majority of Pakistan cricketers in the early Fifties originated. Young stars were picked early as there was a good inter-school competition that culminated in selected teams from one province playing against each other. All these young players were keen to go on and play Test cricket at the Lahore or Dacca Stadium. The final of their event, mostly between Sind and Punjab, was always well contested. These school matches were watched by big crowds and the outstanding performers gained a big reputation, even before they were old enough to start college.

Great help, guidance and coaching was showered on the young school cricketers by the senior club members. In those early years, scouts used to visit the prominent schools in Lahore to locate the bright, young hopes and offer them college places and/or free membership to leading clubs. Playing in the company of senior cricketers and Test players gave early maturity to these young players' game. Government College and Islamia College, Lahore monopolized good players in this way, who then ended up forming the Pakistan team. Aichison College, Lahore produced the great Majid and the famous Imran Khan, who successfully led Pakistan to their World Cup victory over England in Australia two years ago.

Unfortunately, the school cricket system is far less organized now. In the mid-Seventies, all schools except public ones were nationalized. This brought about an explosion in the school-going population and many private schools, run on commercial lines, sprung up in rented residential buildings. Many of these schools have no sports ground or sporting programme and there is also now no coaching system or scouting hierarchy. Yet, despite all these major changes, Pakistan still keeps producing young cricketers with exceptional playing ability, year after year.

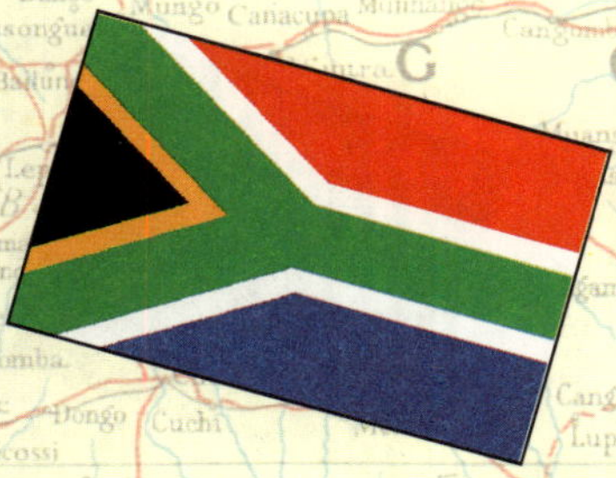

SOUTH AFRICA – *Welcome back to the crease!*

'South African cricket has been sorely missed on the international circuit

This year South Africa toured England for the first time in 29 years. Despite being in exile from the cricketing community they have managed to produce excellent, competitive players. Bowling hero Fanie de Villiers and the strong opening batsman Gary Kirsten have maintained high standards despite virtual isolation.

In the pre-unity years, cricket was run entirely through South African high schools and primary schools, which both had their own Associations. The strength of South African cricket was virtually guaranteed by about 12 schools who annually produced cricketers of an international standard.

Since unity, there has been an important change to cope with the need for first-class players of the future. The junior cricket played in under-privileged areas cannot be left in the hands of an inadequate education system, so it is now run by the clubs in the areas with a township, such as Lange (Cape Town), and Soweto (Johannesburg). These clubs are formed from all the players in their area. As a result, junior cricket for the under-13s and under-19s is now run by Youth Associations with the United Cricket Board. With Youth Associations being the national body, the focus of South African cricket is now the various youth age groups because this is where underprivileged players are first going to make a strong impact. All these ambitious young cricketers hope to go on and represent their country at the famous grounds of Ellis Park in Johannesburg and Newlands in Cape Town.

Representative cricket is played at the under-13 level at an annual inter-provincial week, but no national side is selected at this time. Nevertheless, players such as Rhodes, Cronje and Snell first made their mark at this national week. There is also a regional week for the under-15s, however, where the national side is chosen. It was here that the team that visited England to play the Bunbury/ESCA Tests in 1992 was selected – a sure sign that South African cricket has been sorely missed on the international circuit.

South Africa are lucky that they still have plenty of schoolmasters who have the skills to administer and coach, and there are also England professionals who regularly coach in South Africa. There is no doubt that South African youth cricket is as strong as anywhere else in the world and it will get considerably stronger as their choice of players is broadened.

SRI LANKA – *Sheer grit and dedication*

'There is no doubt that in Sri Lanka the schools feed young players to the national cricket team. It is the outstanding schoolboy cricketer who makes it to the top'

The Colombo Cricket Club in Sri Lanka has hosted many cricket matches which show the young Sri Lankan cricketers the standards they must reach to be a successful Test Match player.

There is no doubt that in Sri Lanka the schools feed talented young players to the national cricket team. It is the outstanding schoolboy cricketer who makes it to the top. The current national skipper Arjuna Ranatunga and his deputy, Aravinda de Silva, made their Test debuts as 18-year-old schoolboys against England in the country's first ever Test in February 1982. It would be difficult to find a national player who did not succeed at school.

In Sri Lanka, school cricket is played at four age-group levels: under-13, under-15, under-17 and under-19 years. In the first category there are about 150 teams; a similar number in the under-15 group, 140 at stage three, while the senior stage includes almost 80 sides. The Sri Lanka Schools' Cricket Association has an annual tournament for the first three age groups, while the senior teams have a much publicized competition, sponsored and run by Coca Cola.

The Schools' Association is run by a dedicated band of school teachers who rely totally on sponsorship, much as in England. These teachers travel to all parts of the island on shoestring budgets, often in their own time, to ensure the national tournaments go well.

Sadly, the Board of Control, despite being directly fed with players for the schools, have always displayed a rather resentful attitude towards the Schools' Association. For instance, any national under-19 team, made up mainly of schoolboys, will be selected by the national selectors, and if the side goes on tour, a school master will find it extremely difficult to accompany the side as an official. The Board of Control sends its own representative. Despite all this, the schools continue to serve the national cause and remain the firm foundation of Sri Lankan cricket.

Tillekaratne has already scored over 1000 Test runs, so the standards have already been set for the players of the future.

WEST INDIES – *Can they be beaten?*

'The standard of cricket at school is so high in the West Indies that Roy Marshall, Gerry Gomez, Jeff Stollmeyer, Clyde Walcott and the great Gary Sobers all played first-class cricket at the age of 16'

There's no doubt that the Windies produce the most exciting and daring fast bowlers in cricket. They also have superb opening batsmen as England's recent tour painfully revealed. To maintain these ridiculously high standards cricket must be played and loved. And it certainly is!

The state of schools' cricket in the West Indies varies from island to island. Barbados has a very high standard. There are three major schools on the island – Lodge School, Harrison College and Combermer School. These schools played in the first division club competition up until the early 70s, so lads up to the age of 19 could play against Test players. A combined schools league of primary, grammar and polytechnic schools was then introduced. In 1985 this league was split into Northern and Southern Divisions, which then competed in the club competition. Desmond Haynes went to Federal School and played his early cricket in the village league. Malcolm Marshall went to Marshall Parkinson school and played in the under-15s.

In Jamaica there is the Sunlight Cup competition, and Guyana and Trinidad also run inter-school competitions. The popular cricketer, Viv Richards, played for Antigua Grammar School and the full Antiguan Island side at just 16.

The standard of cricket at school is so high in the West Indies that the natural players: Roy Marshall, Gerry Gomez, Jeff Stollmeyer, Clyde Walcott and the great Gary Sobers all played first-class cricket at the age of 16. Current Test star Brian Lara went to the Fatima College RC School in Trinidad – home of the world's largest Test ground, the Queen's Park Oval.

The Windward Islands run an inter-school competition of cricket, organized through Grenada, Dominica, St Lucia and St Vincent. Meanwhile, in the keenly contested Sunlight Cup of Jamaica, it was Kingston, Jamaica, Woolmers and Excelsior Colleges who discovered Test stars Jeffrey Dujon, Michael Holding and Courtney Walsh.

On the international schools scene, the Sir Garfield Sobers International Schools Tournament is held in Barbados each summer at the famous Kensington Oval. Schools from England, South Africa and Canada come to test their cricketing skills.

ZIMBABWE – *The new kids on the circuit*

'The competitive nature of the inter-schools matches makes it an excellent training ground for potential stars'

Zimbabwe played their first overseas tour last year. Their Test Match against India was a historic one and showed their rapid progress. Players such as Houghton, (the captain), Flower, Campbell and Ranchod have all come through the ranks to represent their country at the highest level.

Cricket is a fairly major sport in the schools at all levels in Zimbabwe. It is played in public and private schools, and competition on the field starts at a very young age. Children get involved in inter-school competitions at around 8 or 9 years of age and can play up to 20 games a year. The first important national selection is for the 'Colts', the under-12s, just finishing primary school. The Colts tour Zimbabwe and can sometimes tour abroad.

Once into secondary school, inter-school competitions increase greatly and there are often school tours, which are sponsored by the school, parents and companies. However, due to Zimbabwe's location, international tours are expensive. The next national selection is for the Fawns, the under-15s, and much effort is put into getting this team abroad. It's at this level that potential top-class cricketers are first noticed. The final national selection of school cricketers is for the Nuffield XI, the under-18s. These boys start playing in the National League, which has between 7–10 sides. The Zimbabwean Cricket Union also helps out by sponsoring a broad coaching package aimed at helping local players, which is often supported by takings from touring funds, World Cup participation and money raising.

The sunny weather in Zimbabwe is ideal for cricket and easy access in schools to cricket fields and nets. The competitive nature in inter-schools' matches makes it an excellent training ground for potential stars. However, this has not been matched by the international exposure a player receives in his later school years. Yet this has improved with South Africa coming back into the game. Lately, many of Zimbabwe's finest players have gone abroad and made their mark in another country. Now that Test Status has been introduced, Zimbabwe's youth are more encouraged to stay.

Although the player base in Zimbabwe is small when compared to other Test nations, commitment and enthusiasm for the game among the country's youth goes a long way to ensuring Zimbabwe's status as a Test cricketing nation.

CAUGHT OUT!

Quinten Quenches!

Harper and the Bird

Where's Noddy?

Gary Headley and Mike Gatting

CAUGHT OUT!

Essex man and Welsh rarebit

'Sinton simmers'

Gunners signs for Bunbury!

Rolling Stone meets the Four Tops

HISTORY IN THE MAKING

The South Africa under 15 Team, Finchley, August '92.

The Bunbury/ESCA (English Schools Cricket Association) Festival is the most important week for under 15-year-old cricketers in England. Over the last 26 years, all the great players have been 'discovered' during this annual event, including: David Gower, Mike Gatting, Graham Gooch, Mike Atherton, Ian Botham and Gary Lineker!

To qualify for the Bunbury Festival, every cricketer has to play firstly for a school team, then their county, before being selected for their region, be it North, South, West or Midlands.

In recent years, John Crawley has worked his way through to go on to play for Lancashire and the England A teams. So did Ben Smith (Leicestershire CCC) and Ronnie Irani (Lancashire CCC). Extraordinarily, Ian Botham, the most festive of all cricketers, slipped through the net and was not chosen for the final England side. However, his son, Liam, was selected for the England under-15 team to play against South Africa in the first ever schoolboy Test series between England and South Africa. The under-15 team were the first national cricket side to come out of South Africa since the easing of apartheid.

In 1991 when South Africa was readmitted to world cricket, Cyril Cooper and I went to meet Dr Ali Bacher, Chairman of the United Cricket Board of South Africa. Cyril was then the General Secretary of ESCA. We had a common ambition – to give as many young people as possible the opportunity to play and enjoy cricket at the highest level, while seeing the world at the same time.

With the adrenalin pumping, Cyril and I arrived at The Westbury Hotel to meet Ali Bacher. He had been jogging and was wearing shorts. It didn't help to relax us. 'Come inside and tell me your plans,' he calmly said. When we had finished, there was a seemingly endless silence. Dr Bacher then rose to his feet. 'Fantastic!' he boomed. We had found a kindred spirit, and within the space of 10 minutes the ground-breaking tour had been confirmed.

On August 3 1992, a South African cricket team played in England for the first time in 27 years. The South Africans had assembled a multi-racial squad which had been picked on merit. All the provinces in SA had nominated their best lads. The players' backgrounds were vastly different.

It was fitting that the first game would be against the Prime Minister's XI at Finchley Cricket Club. Mr Major, a great supporter of cricket, ESCA and Bunbury, had felt it important to establish a valuable link with the new South Africa through the first game of the tour.

At Finchley, the South Africans struggled in the cold, blustery conditions, but fiercely defended a modest total before losing with just two balls remaining. It was hard to believe that the players on the field were only 15 years of age. Fast bowler David Terbrugge, 6ft 3in tall from Johannesburg, tore into the English batsmen with some hostile deliveries, as did Andile Mzenge. Mark Benfield resembled the great Barry Richards in appearance, and also in the style he stroked his way to a stylish 54. Only a mature 72 from England's Philip Ayres and a determined 31 from Tom Newham ensured an English victory.

The relationship between the two teams was exceptional. During long breaks caused by rain, impromptu games of baseball and touch rugby involving all the players, revealed the best in camaraderie and spontaneity. The banter and leg-pulling between the boys helped to build friendship with team-mates and the opposition alike. The day Liam Botham from Yorkshire was made an honorary Zulu by Gift Pedi from Bloemfontein will remain in my memory forever.

Just imagine if all the different nations came together. Today, South Africa, tomorrow the world?

The South African Ambassador Kent Durr meets the South African Team at Finchley. Gift Pedi in the foreground looking glum.

£700,000 NOT OUT!

The Leukaemia Virus Centre in Glasgow has benefited greatly from funds generated by Ian Botham's long, sponsored walks, and a building at the centre is named after him.

When playing our Bunbury cricket games people ask me, 'Where does all the money raised actually go to?' Since the year 1986, the celebrity Bunburys have managed to raise over £700,000 for various charities and other worthwhile causes. Over the years we have given our support to the Leukaemia Research Fund, Mencap, Childline, Wishes, the Royal Marsden Hospital, the Cystic Fibrosis Trust, the Bryan Robson Scanner Appeal, Riding for the Disabled, the Arthritis Council, Multiple Sclerosis, the Playing Field Association and Stoke Mandeville Hospital. Many other cricketers' benefit appeals have also been included and of course not forgetting the important English Schools Cricket Association.

A Bunbury game at Godmersham in 1993 raised more then £20,000 for the Leukaemia Research fund. This is the only national charity concerned solely with leukaemia and related blood disorders in children and adults. Acting on the impartial advice of independent experts, the fund initiates and supports research covering the cancers of the blood and other diseases. Running costs at the Leukaemia Research Fund are low because 95 pence on every £1 goes directly to the fund's comprehensive research programme. The Leukaemia Research Fund runs nine specialist research centres and units nationwide, often using funds raised at sporting events such as the Bunbury cricket matches.

The regular Bunbury game at Alconbury versus Norma Major's cricketing XI in aid of Mencap is always one of the happiest events on the fixture list. All the biggest stars have played for the Bunburys in this particular game, including Gary Lineker, Imran Khan, David Essex, Rory Bremner and Indian test captain Mohammad Azharudin.

The biggest handicap facing anyone with a learning disability is the attitude of other people.

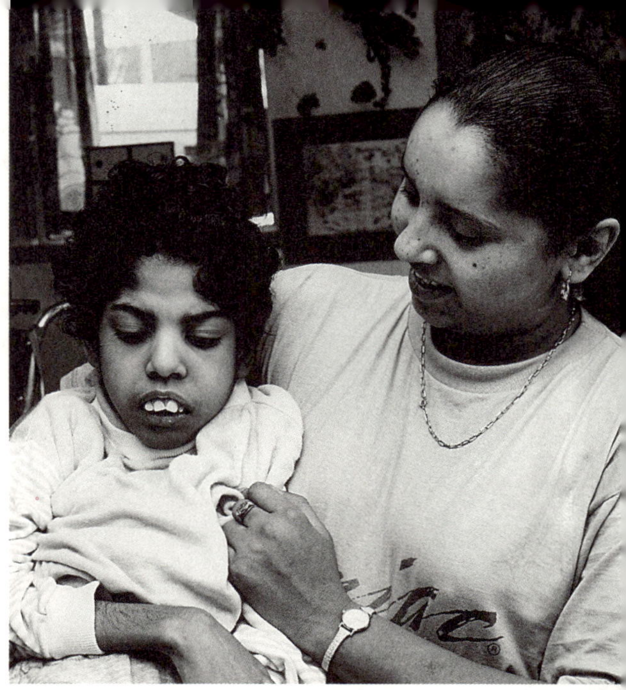

Formed in 1946 as a parent action group, Mencap has grown to be the UK's largest voluntary organization for people with learning disabilities. The Mencap message is simple: people with disabilities have the same basic rights as anyone else – to be part of the community, to develop their abilities to the full and to be accepted as people in their own right, with individual talents and needs. Like all charities, Mencap depends particularly on the generosity of their supporters. Without this tremendous support, their valued work could not continue.

Childline is the only free helpline in Britain for children in trouble or danger. Childline's primary aim is to listen to children and to advise, comfort and protect them. Around 10,000 attempted calls from children to Childline's freephone 0800 1111 number are logged by BT's automatic counter every day. Of these 10,000 calls, Childline answer 2,000 a day – a number which is slowly, but steadily, increasing. Childline's goal is to be able to answer every child's call first time, but to do so they need funds to pay for more phone lines and to train more volunteer counsellors. The Bunbury Childline match at the Oval in 1993 raised over £20,000 to help meet this need.

Childline aims to help children in distress 24 hours a day, every day of the year.

ChildLine

0800 1111

SO YOU THINK YOU'VE GOT PROBLEMS!

WORST TEST FIGURES

The distinction of achieving the worst bowling figures in Test match history goes to the hitherto unsung L.O.B. 'Chuck' Fleetwood-Smith, an Australian left-arm spinner. Playing against England at the Oval in 1938, his sustained spell didn't exactly succeed in tying the home bats down. England declared at 903-7 and Fleetwood-Smith finished with the highly forgettable figures of 1-298.

TOO SMALL FOR HIS BOOTS

Even the greatest of players have their off days. Take Denis Compton about to make his MCC debut against Suffolk at Felixstowe. Later renowned for being not exactly the most organised of individuals, young Compton arrived at the ground to discover that he had left his cricket bag at Lord's. Consequently, he was obliged to take the field in kit borrowed from a player seven inches taller than himself and who took two-and-a-half-boot sizes larger. The suspicion that Compton would have been more comfortable in a suit of armour was reinforced when, scarcely able to move about the crease, he was not altogether surprisingly bowled first ball.

ILLUSTRIOUS CAREER

When the great Australian cricketers are under discussion, for some reason it is always the likes Bradman, Benaud and Lillee that spring to the fore. Only rarely does that of Dr R.L. Park warrant a mention. Perhaps this is because in his solitary Test appearance against England at Melbourne in 1920, the hapless medic was out first ball in his only innings and delivered a solitary over which cost his side nine runs. He was said to be disappointed at not being selected again.

TEST MATCH (2 players)

Deal all the cards face down on the table apart from the ***Al Caprawn*** card. Take it in turns to flip over two cards at a time face up. Whenever they match, keep them in your pile. If they don't match, turn them all down again, and the next player tries.

The winner is the lucky person with the most cards, in pairs, when all of the cards have been removed from the table.

CAPRAWN'S CASINO (3 to 5 players)

The object is to get rid of all your cards – but try not to get stuck with the dastardly ***Al Caprawn***. Deal out all the cards. Players set down any pairs they have face up on the table.

Then the player on the dealer's left holds out his cards face-down to the player on his left, who picks one of them, and so on. Anytime you get a pair, set it down on the table. When all the cards have been paired off, you're safely out of the game. The loser is the one left holding the ***Al Caprawn*** card.

Machine Bun Kelly

Dogfather

Radish

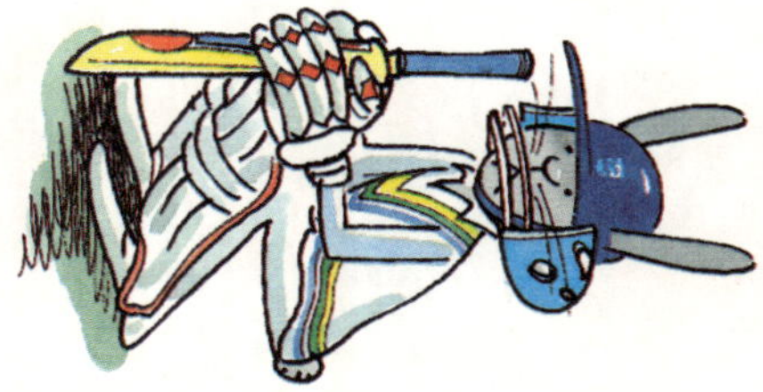

Atherbun

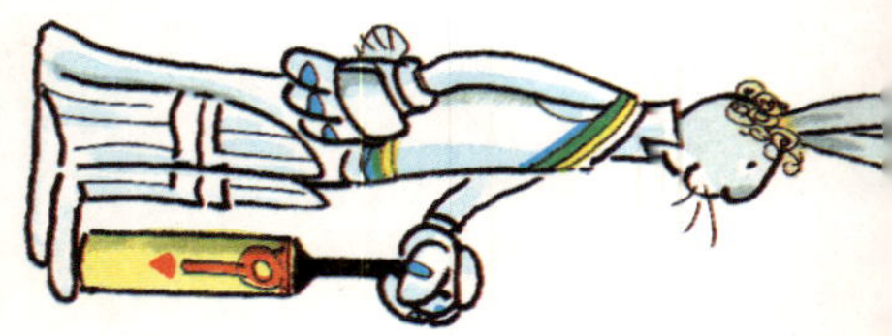

Goldenhare

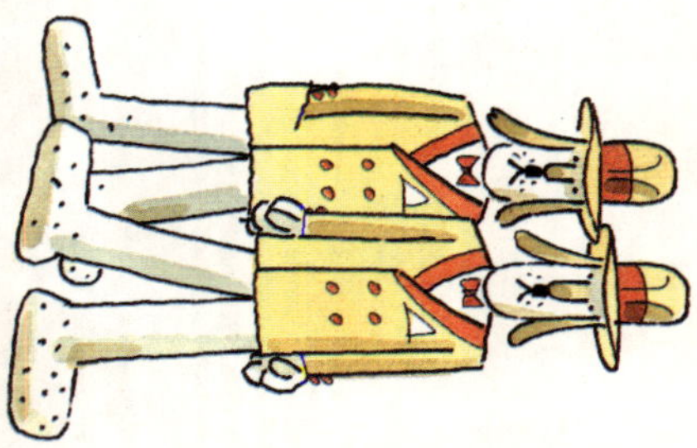

Ronnie & Reggie Krayhound

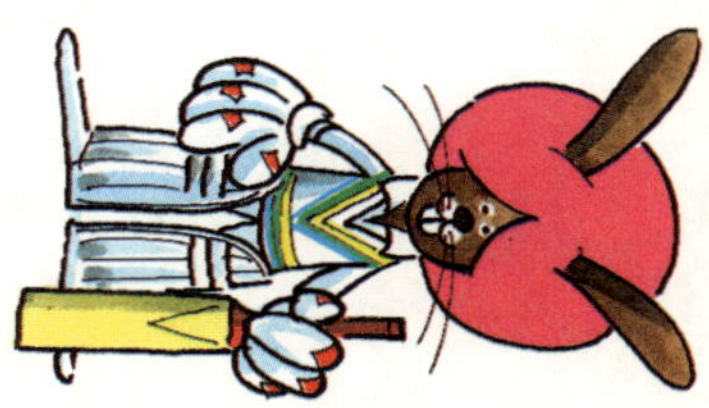

Rajbun

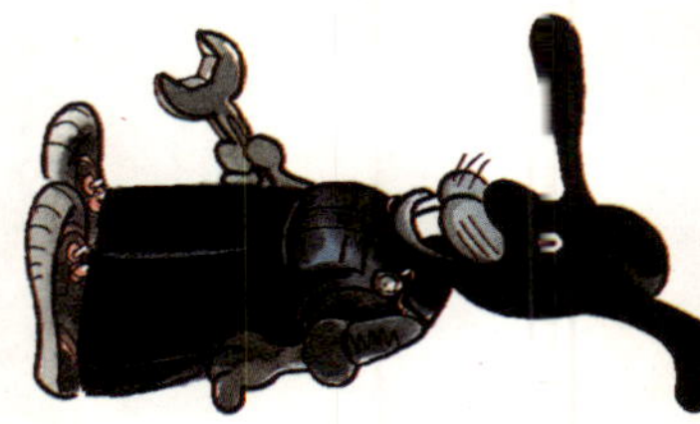

Greasebun

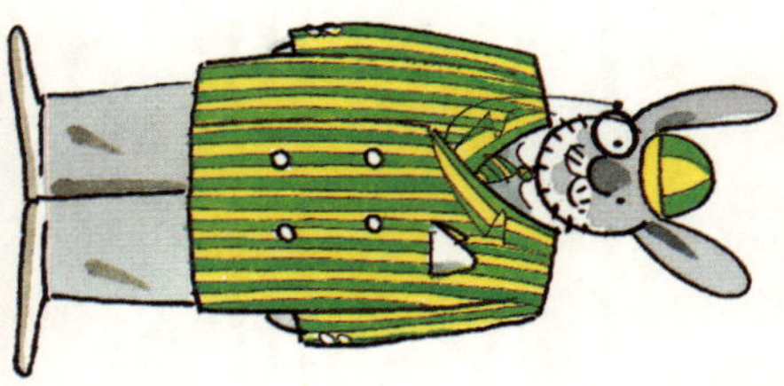

Old Holbun

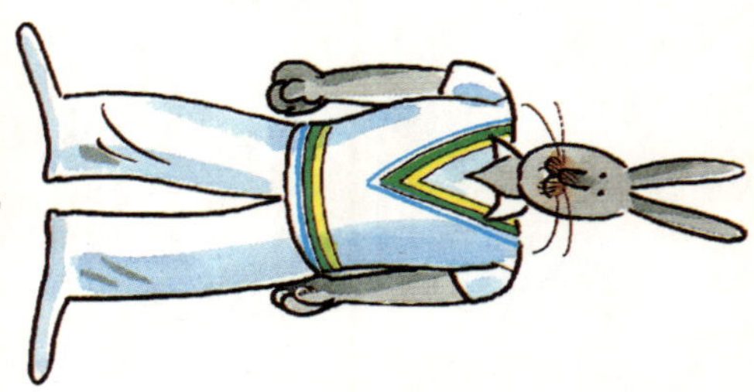

Buntham

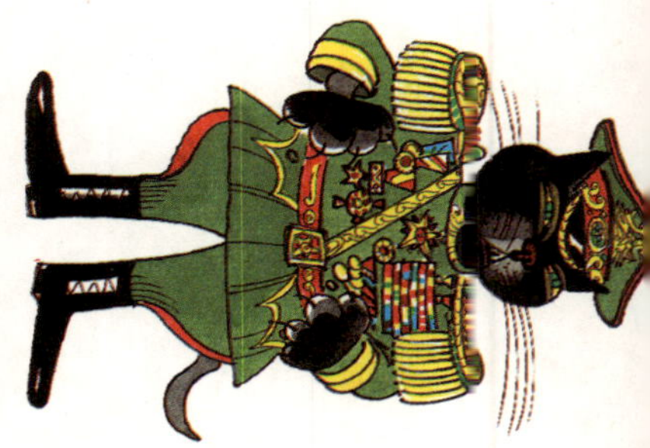

Katman of Kathmandu

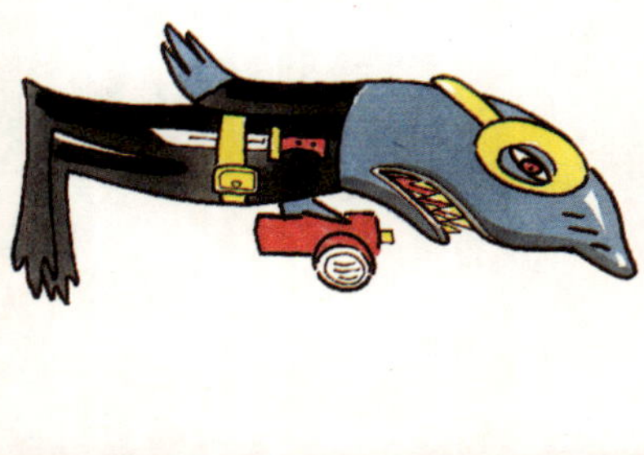

Shark Cousteau

Atilla the Bun

Anna Conda

Dogfather

Goldenhare

Greasebun

Katman of Kathmandu

Anna Conda

Machine Bun Kelly

Atherbun

Rajbun

Buntham

Atilla the Bun

BUNBURYS

BUNBURYS
BUNBURYS
BUNBURYS
BUNBURYS
BUNBURYS
BUNBURYS
BUNBURYS
BUNBURYS
BUNBURYS
BUNBURYS
BUNBURYS
BUNBURYS
BUNBURYS
BUNBURYS

SO YOU THINK YOU'VE GOT PROBLEMS!

GREEN'S HOUSE EFFECT

When Walsden entertained Rochdale in a Central Lancashire League match, Walsden bowler Peter Green was hit for a massive six by Rochdale batsman Wilson Hartley. The ball sailed out of the ground and smashed through the window of a house in an adjoining street. To add insult to injury, it was Peter Green's house.

BURNT OUT

Batting at Kalgoorie, Australia, in the 1970s, one Stan Dawson was struck by a speedy delivery that promptly ignited a box of matches which he had secreted in his hip pocket. To add to his woe, Dawson was run out as he tried to beat down the flames.

HASTY EXIT

England's 1959-60 tour of the West Indies was marred by disgraceful riot scenes in Port of Spain. Bottles and seats were hurled onto the pitch, observed by the keen eye of BBC radio commentator Rex Alston. 'I've never seen anything like this is my life,' he broadcasted. 'The crowd away to my right are behaving like a lot of hooligans.' Unfortunately for Alston, the said crowd were tuned in to his commentary on their transistor radios and on hearing his words of condemnation, they turned towards the derelict commentary box in anger. Alston and his colleagues were forced to flee to safety as the old box was reduced to a pile of rubbish in little more than 30 seconds.

MORBID SCORECARD

Playing in the final of the 1958-59 Qaid-I-Azam Trophy in Karachi, Abul Aziz was injured in the first innings. The scorecard thus read: 'Abdul Aziz retired hurt ....0.' The injury proved to be fatal and the scorer, obviously not wishing to leave any room for doubt, wrote for the second innings 'Abdul Aziz did not bat, dead....0'.

...CONTINUED FROM PAGE 44

BEATEN BY A BUNCH OF BUNNIES...
I DON'T THINK WE'RE GOOD ENOUGH...
..I WANT REVENGE MIAOW!
NOT GOOD ENOUGH! GET ME PROFESSOR WHISKERS!
COME ON PROFESSOR I WANT RESULTS!
...OFF WENT PROF. WHISKERS!

MEANTIME, BACK IN BUNBURY, THE TEAM WERE PREPARING FOR THE GAME AGAINST GRAHAM POOCH, ALLAN BOUNDER, CURTLY HAMBONE AND THE REST OF BARKING C.C.
LOOK AT FRANCES EDBUNS IN THE BUGLE!
BUNBURY BUGLE

HE'S CALLED HATTRICK CATTERSON DO YOU KNOW HIM VIV..?
BUNBURY BUGLE
WHISKERTOWN SIGNS OVERSEAS STAR TO DEFEAT BUNBURYS
E. MOGG PAYS FORTUNE
NO MAN, CAN'T SAY I'VE HEARD OF HIM..!!
PATRICK TWITCHFIELD AND THE PAPACAZZI WERE AT CATWICK TO MEET HATTRICK CATTERSON
CATWICK AIRPORT
BUNNYBADOS AIR
I'VE COME TO MAKE WHISKERTOWN THE TOP CATS. WE'RE GOING TO WHOP THOSE BUNBURYS!

CONTINUED ON PAGE 90...

THE BAD GUYS

These are the cunning adversaries who will do anything to get one over on the cricketing good guys

A canine American. Born in a litter bin, Tony Pepperoni grew up in the socio-economically deprived Hell's Kitchen area of New York. His father was a gangland boss, Vito 'wet nose' Pepperoni, who emigrated to America from a small village in Sicily. It is said he had to flee for his life following a vendetta involving two donkeys and a crow. The true facts are not known, but it was rumoured to have been a matter of honour. In 1968 Vito was sentenced to 96 billion years' imprisonment for unpaid parking tickets. A week later, Tony took over the dog biscuit business. But when some of the other gangland bosses tried to muscle in, it led to a famous gangland war which only ended when Tony pulled off a master stroke by rubbing out all his opponents with an eraser. After all, what better way is there to get rid of unwanted cartoon characters?

The Dogfather is cruel, intelligent, and completely devious. He is suspected of being the head of an international ring of crooks and assorted scallywags, and he's said to have at least a dozen judges in his pocket. This can only mean one of two things – members of the legal profession are getting smaller, or he wears really big trousers.

TONY PEPPERONI A.K.A THE DOGFATHER

AL CAPRAWN

A real heavy. A fat and oily character with a short temper – it lasts about 10 seconds. Head of the East Coast syndicate, Al is a flamboyant character who loves getting the attention of the media. Usually if he sees any reporters he draws his Colt 45 and takes a pot shot at them – which usually gets their full attention.

Nicknamed 'Scar' because of the prominent scar on his left cheek – unfortunately you can't see it because it's on the left cheek of his bum. Not as brilliant as the Dogfather, Al Caprawn often acts on impulse.

MACHINE BUN KELLY

A reputed hitman in Al Caprawn's syndicate, Machine Bun Kelly made his reputation by breaking out of Sing Sing prison in 1957. It was a remarkable escape . . . not only was he just 8 years old at the time, he had to break in first! But then that's typical of Kelly. Most of the time he's out to lunch. A psychological evaluation described him as being a *cerebro-atmospheric* individual – which is basically a technical term for an 'airhead'.

On his hits, Kelly uses a specially modified Thompson sub-machine gun, which fires miniature salami sausages, Parmesan cheese, and olives. This is the reason why his victims end up looking like pizzas. It has also led to the introduction of the term: *'being deep panned'*.

KATMAN OF KATHMANDU

This is a most terrible cat who lives in The Place of the Winds. The name is derived from the Katman's favourite food – curried beans. Here this most awful person is surrounded by his Bungal tigers. They are all man-eaters – which is why the male population in Kathmandu are all wearing ladies' clothes.

There is a heartrending and most tragic story that the Katman wanted a son to carry on his most tyrannical rule, but that his wife gave birth to a daughter called Rose Patel. The cruel-hearted Katman immediately disowned the baby and his wife was never seen again . . . They also say that the Katman works for the evil Dogfather and has faithfully promised to destroy the great Bunburys.

ATILLA THE BUN

Atilla is a real scoundrel and a backstabbing henchman for the Katman, who is often seen driving around in a *Sahib Turbon*. He has a failed degree in Archaeology from the University of Bombay, and he became famous when he wrote the book, *Indian Bones in the Temple of Gloom*. Unlike the Katman, Atilla is a coward at heart and is quick to change sides when the going gets tough.

SHARK COUSTEAU

Cousteau is apparently involved in the nutcotics trade. This is a very lucrative business as there are people willing to pay a fortune for salted cashews or roast monkey nuts.

You cannot miss Cousteau. He has a mouth like a JCB digger, large, sharp teeth and horrible black eyes.The most recent sighting of Cousteau was three years ago when he called into a public swimming bath for lunch – and ate 43 bathers. This is probably the reason why he does not mix well with other people. One rumour circulating in the underworld was that he had invited a *gill* friend to his flat for dinner. Unfortunately, it turned out to be true.

ANNA CONDA

The above person is presently on the *Police Hissing List*. It is suspected that she may be the Dogfather's girlfriend as she seems to spend a lot of time at his mansion. Little is known about her, although we think she may have been the brains behind some of his big capers.

Described as cunning, sly and treacherous, Anna Conda once had a big crush on the Krayhound brothers . . . and ended up cracking three of their ribs.

RONNIE AND REGGIE KRAYHOUND

Born to Ethel Krayhound, housewife and bingo caller, and Albert Krayhound, unemployed harmonica tuner, in Essex. They both attended Magpie Comprehensive and left with 3 'A' Levels each, two typewriters, 50 textbooks and a folding chair.

The Krayhounds are presently employed as bodyguards and general assistants to the Dogfather. They're said to be totally loyal to their employer – even when he loses his temper and runs them over with a 50-ton steamroller.

The Bad Guys are also featured in their own adventures – see page 94 for details

BUNNYBADOS

Skipper Buntham and his heroes had just pipped Whiskertown in the Bunson and Hedges, Cat West Final. A national holiday had been declared by the hare to the throne and Bunbury was officially named a Royal Burrow.

As Buntham held the trophy aloft for all to see, he smiled. *'Now we must take on the rest of the world, starting with the Caribun island of Bunnybados. Get your passports ready, lads, we're off on Saturday!'*

'Can I come skipper?' enquired young Rajbun.

'I'm sorry, son, not this time, you're too young. You must go home and look after your mum and dad – your touring days with the team will come all in good time.'

Old Holbun announced the touring party. There would be changes. Viv Radish would be playing for his native Bunnybados. Bunny Buntham would take a well-earned rest from the captaincy and the new skipper would be Goldenhare Gower. He had batted well and deserved his chance. Mike Brer-ley would be the team manager and he had decided to include Allan Ram and Graham Pooch to add power to the batting. Umpire for the trip was going to be Dickie Purred of Paradise.

The official photograph showed a very impressive team of bunnies.

Bidding farewell to their loved ones, the Bunbury XI set sail on SS *Buncan Fearnley* and chugged slowly in a westward direction to the twinkling Caribun Islands.

'*This is the life, buoys,*' said Goldenhare, stretched out on his sun lounger. Then, just as he was about to fall asleep, a voice in his ear almost made him jump out of his skin.

'*Excuse me Mr Gower, my name is Captain Tom Kitten and I am in charge of this ship. I wondered if you and your party would like to take on the ship's cats to keep you in shape?*'

'*Delighted, we're ready when you are!*' chortled Goldenhare.

Some of the cats in the ship's crew were very good at batting. Could they win by a whisker? Buntham discovered it was not so easy to bowl when the ship was in motion.

Petty Officer McMogg cracked one ball high into the azure sky.

'Go cat! Go!' he cried to his partner, Bosun Pussinboats.

Holiday-makers and deck cats alike watched its flight – up and up – and then, just as it began to fall, a seagull soaring above the ship's wake swooped and took the ball cleanly in its beak.

'Great catch!' gasped Thumpage. *'What's your name?'*

'Martin . . . Martin Crowe,' replied the bird. *'I was just on my way to a fancy-dress party. Do you like my seagull costume?'*

As he spoke, the ball dropped out of his mouth – 'plop!' – straight into a lifeboat.

Cat Furry, the ship's cordon bleu and occasional French cricketer, sprang quickly into the boat to retrieve the ball.*'Ooh! La! La! What 'ave we 'ere?'*

The bunnies rushed to see what he had found.

There, snuggled up in the boat, fast asleep, was Rajbun.

'I can't believe it!' gasped Goldenhare. *'We have a stowaway!'*

'I just wanted to be part of the team,' said Rajbun sadly.

'Don't be too cross with him,' pleaded Buntham.

'There are no boats back to England,' declared Goldenhare. *'Rajbun must come with us to Bunnybados. Ian, you can be responsible for him.'*

'It'll be a pleasure,' smiled Buntham.

The days passed as the big ship sailed across the ocean.

'What a glorious voyage,' wrote Pooch on his postcard home.

'Time for practice,' ordered Goldenhare, putting aside his book, *Warren Peace. 'Everyone on deck.'*

Buntham was bowling to Bob Tailer. Whack! The ball went right over the side of the ship.

'Now we've gone and lost it,' lamented Jackrabbit.

'No! No!' cried Rajbun. *'We've found another fielder out in the deep.'*

There, slipping in and out of the waves, was a dolphin, silvery swift, glistening in the sun and flipping the ball onto the end of his nose. Behind him, twisting and turning, were 10 of his friends.

'Come out and play with us!' called Dolly Vera the dolphin.

The bunnies fastened their cricket bats together with their team ties, and made them into a raft.

'Prepare to launch the SS Buntiki,' roared the bunnies. Over the side they leapt with their raft, which went 'plop!' into the blue sea. Using stumps as paddles, they soon reached the dolphins.

The dolphins gave the bunnies a ride on their backs: racing with the current on the crest of the wave and then going 'whoosh!' down the other side.

'It's just like being on a roller coaster!' screamed Graham Burrow.

Returning them safely to the ship, the dolphins wished their friends farewell.

'Good luck in Bunnybados, boys, you'll certainly need it.'

That night, as the team slept, Goldenhare and Buntham stood by the ship's rail. The ocean was just like glass, sparkling and glistening under a star-spangled sky.

'It will be funny playing against Viv this time,' mused Buntham.

'Yes, but there's no time for sentiment, Ian, we must play to win!' replied Goldenhare.

Early next morning the Bunbury team were awoken by the sound of steel drums beating a calypso rhythm.

'Wake up bunnies, we've arrived,' shouted Captain Tom. *'You seem to have a guard of honour.'*

Sure enough, the ship had moored in a sleepy lagoon and a flotilla of little boats with rainbow-coloured sails had come out to greet the arriving cricketers.

First one up the rope-ladder was Viv Radish. *'Welcome to Bunnybados, man. Hop onto my catamaran and I'll take you ashore.'*

On the beach, the local girls heaped garlands of flowers on the surprised bunnies.

'This is paradise,' sang the Bunbury players.

'Viv, it's so good to see you again,' beamed Buntham embracing his pal.

'Ya man, but I have bad news for you. Unfortunately, the Test ground was flooded by an overnight storm. So we will have to play on the beach.'

'No problem, Viv,' said Buntham.

Changing behind palm trees, the team watched the pretty girls sway by on their way to market with their baskets on their heads.

Viv decided to place the bunnies at the mercy of the two fastest bowlers in the whole of the Caribun Islands: Curtly Hambone and Joel Giraffe.

'Where has he gone?' enquired a puzzled Goldenhare, taking guard in front of the stumps. Curtly's run was so long that he had completely disappeared into nearby Flamboyant Avenue. He went back as far as the chameleon who acted as a traffic light by day, changing from red to green, and a stand-up chameleon by night.

Green! Off sprang Curtly. Down Sandy Lane he galloped, through the crowd, behind the pedalos, past the palms, bounding along the beach at 200 mph. And 'umph!' – he let go of the ball, which parted Goldenhare's curly locks.

'Wow! What a surprise,' gasped the Bunbury skipper, *'I thought he'd gone on his holidays. Send me a postcard!'*

Bunbury were 72 for 3 when Ian Buntham strode onto the beach to join his captain.

Up to the wicket thundered Curtly Hambone, and the ball left his hand like a flash of lightning. Buntham summoned up all his strength and smashed it back with his bat over his head straight into a palm tree – and 14 spectators fell out!

There was pure bedlam: hooters blaring, drums banging, cans clanging and people singing.

Buntham scored 74 before he was bowled out. He had tried his favourite shot, a reverse sweep, but had missed the ball by a hare's breadth. Bunbury were all out for a total of 340, but Captain Goldenhare Gower was cheered into the beach hut, not out for 156.

After some refreshments of lettuce, milk and bananas, Bunbury took the field.

'Right, this is where the fun starts,' exclaimed Goldenhare.

Gordon Greengage and Desmond's *'Got a Barrow'* Haynes opened the batting for Bunnybados. They soon had the Bunbury fielders chasing the ball to all parts of the island. The Bunburys' best bowlers, Edbuns and Emberbunny, sweated profusely under the hot sun.

High up in the palms, Richie Bunaud and Bunny Johnston were commentating for the Bunbury Broadcasting Corporation.

'The sky here is so blue that it may never have held rain,' mumbled Bunny Johnston, his mouth full of melting chocolate cake.

After lunch, in came King Viv. The first ball he received he knocked through the covers for four runs.

'Here we go,' sighed Goldenhare. *'Viv's up to his old tricks!'*

Then, with his score on 49, Viv played his famous pull shot straight into a palm tree. This colossal blow loosened the coconuts and one fell, landing on the head of Thumpage. Up until then he had been enjoying fielding in the shade.

Seeing stars, Thumpage hurled it at the wicket-keeper. Bob Tailer whipped off the bails. Viv was run out by a yard. All the bunnies ran to congratulate Thumpage, who by now lay in a heap on the sand.

'Great throw, eh, Dickie?' cried Goldenhare.

'Yes,' replied Dickie Purred. *'But you'd better help me find the ball, that was a coconut he threw in!'*

'I've got a lovely bunch of coconuts!' sang the ecstatic crowd.

'Bring on our 12th man,' boomed Buntham.

Out strolled a proud Rajbun, his ears popping out of the sunhat perched on his turban.

It was the final over and Bunnybados needed six to win. Motorists coming home from work pulled their cars over to the roadside to hear the final moments of the match on their radios.

In ran Buntham. Viv took a mighty swing sending the ball miles out into the lagoon.

'It's mine!' cried Rajbun, diving into the sea and swimming for all he was worth.

The spectators at the water's edge held their breaths as the ball went up and up. Would it never come down? Rajbun swam faster and faster. It wasn't possible that the little rabbit could catch it – surely?

At last the ball began its descent. Suddenly Rajbun was lifted through the surf and grabbed the ball.

What a catch! Viv couldn't believe it.

'Well caught Rajbun!' cried his team-mates with glee.

'Well, I couldn't have done it without a little help from my friends,' laughed the young hero.

There, to everyone's astonishment, was Dolly the dolphin. He had hoisted Rajbun out of the sea with a twitch of his shiny nose.

Bunbury had won!

The festivities went on late into the night. The bunnies danced to Bucks Fizz, Bunny Wailer and Echo and the Bunnymen.

'We needn't watch the television this evening,' laughed Richie Bunaud. *'If we want to see the highlights, we can look at Buntham's new hairdo!'*

The scent of flowers and happy sounds of laughter and music were still high on the wind as the SS *Buncan Fearnley* steamed out of Bunnybados the next morning.

'Cheerio Viv! Cheerio lads!' waved all the bunnies.

...CONTINUED FROM PAGE 74

YOU LOOK A BIT OFF COLOUR HATTRICK!
DON'T YOU LIKE THE RAIN?
SURE ENOUGH THE BLACK CAT HAD BECOME A GINGER TOM.
WHISKERTOWN
275 FOR 2 DEC.
H. CATTERSON
180 N.O.
I CAN'T BELIEVE IT..!
..TO HIS DISBELIEF OLD HOLBUN SPOTTED THE HEADLINES OF THE AFTERNOON'S PAPER
AFTERNOON NEWS
OVERSEAS CRICKET STAR HATTRICK CATTERSON TO OPEN NEW BRANCH OF HABICAT IN MOUSEWELL HILL AT 3.30 P.M.

ONE MINUTE, IF HATTRICK IS IN MOUSEWELL HILL, WHO THE HELL IS THAT OUT THERE?
BEFORE CHAIRMAN MIAOW COULD EXPLAIN, THE RAIN STARTED AGAIN. HATTRICK CATTERSON WAS STRIDING TO THE WICKET...
WHEN HE WAS SUDDENLY STRUCK BY A FLASH OF LIGHTNING. THE CAT LIT UP, HIS HEAD FLEW OFF HIS SHOULDERS AND HIS SHOULDERS AND HIS ARM LEFT ITS SOCKET AND WENT FLYING THROUGH THE AIR!

CRASH!
STRAIGHT THROUGH THE COMMITTEE ROOM WINDOW!
HE WAS AN IDENTICAT!
...YOU SEE HE WASN'T REAL, BUT A MACHINE BUILT BY PROF. WHISKERS
THE REAL HATTRICK CATTERSON IS AN ORDINARY CRICKETER. PROF. WHISKERS MADE A MECHANICAL CAT BASED ON A BOWLING MACHINE PRINCIPLE, TO RESEMBLE CATTERSON ON MATCH DAYS...
FROM FRANCES EDBUN

JUST THEN THE DOOR BURST OPEN - IN WALKED HAT-TRICK CATTERSON WITH A BUNNY GIRL ON EACH ARM!
HOW DID THE GAME GO, BOSS?
ERNEST MOGG DIDN'T ANSWER FOR THE SECOND TIME THAT DAY. THE WHISKERTOWN PRESIDENT WAS TO COLLAPSE TO THE FLOOR...
HATTRICK PATTERSON WAS NEVER TO BE SEEN AGAIN. AS FOR HIS MECHANICAL PARTNER, HE STILL REMAINS IN PIECES R.I.P. (RUST IN THE PAVILION.)

...LET'S ORGANIZE A CHARITY WALK!
CHARITY WALK
THE GREATER THE VOLUME THE BIGGER PAYDAY
I WONDER WHO WILL HAVE THE BIGGEST LOAD..!
...I WILL SHOW THEM..!!

...IF YOU'LL MAKE IT TO THE END, YOU'LL BE A HERO!

...WE HAVE LIFT-OFF!

THE FAMOUS ALL CONQUERING BUNBURYS RECEIVED MANY REQUESTS TO PLAY AROUND THE WORLD.
RRRING! RRRING! RRRING!
INVITATIONS
FOR OUR WORLD TOUR WE WILL NEED TRANSPORT. GENTLEMEN MEET OUR NEW MECHANIC GREASEBUN FROM BROOKLYN!
HE HAS RECENTLY BEEN WORKING DAY AND NIGHT AND HAS A SURPRISE FOR US...!

...ARE YOU READY FOR THIS..?!
WELCOME TO THE BUNNYMOBILE!

BUNBURY CLUB MERCHANDISE

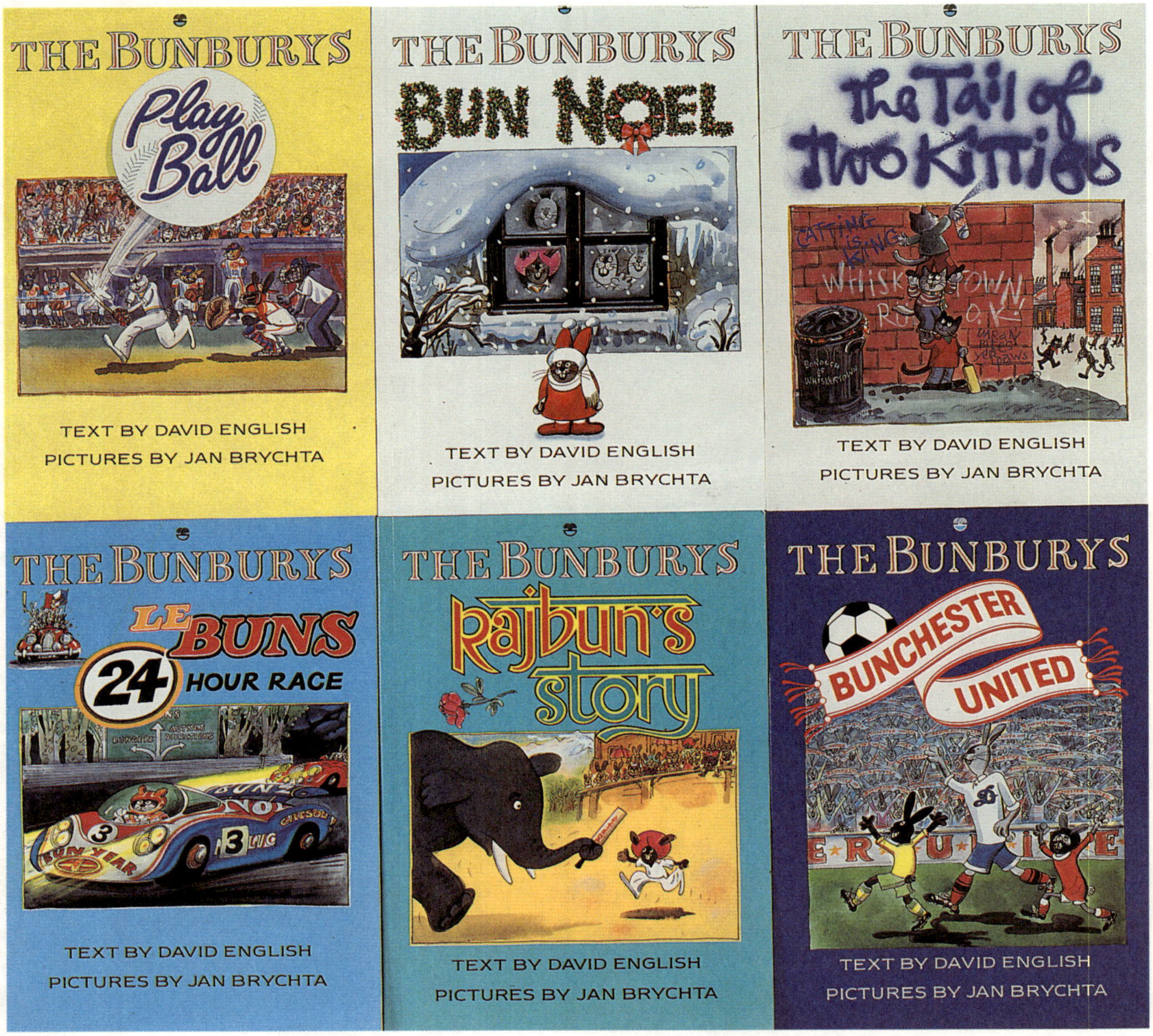

BOOKS AVAILABLE

Bun Noel foreword by Ian Botham
£3.99 + 40p postage

Bunchester United foreword by Bobby Robson
£3.99 + 40p postage

Play Ball foreword by Tommy Lasorda, manager of LA Dodgers World Champs 1988
£3.95 + 40p postage

A Tail of Two Kitties foreword by Mike Gatting
£3.95 + 40p postage

Le Buns 24 Hour Race
foreword by Graham Dilley
£3.99 + 40p postage

Rajbun's Story foreword by David Gower
£3.99 + 40p postage

SWEATSHIRTS

Children sizes 26/28, 30/32,
£9.99 + 70p postage
Adult sizes small and medium only
£12 + 70p postage

BUNBURY WHITE SUN HAT

£11.99 + 43p postage
£11.99 + 36p postage

TEESHIRTS

Children sizes 22/24, 26/28, 30/32,
£7.50 + 36p postage
XXL Big and Baggy Bunbury Teeshirt
£11.99 + 36p postage

BUNBURY SLEEVELESS ADULT SWEATER

sizes small, medium, large, XL
£18.50 + 70p postage

BUNBURY SLEEVED ADULT SWEATER

sizes small, medium, large, XL
£19.50 + 70p postage

BUNBURY GREEN SUN HAT

£11.99 + 43p postage

Please send cheques to:
The Bunbury Cricket Club
P.O. Box 3429
London NW7 4JQ

ACKNOWLEDGEMENTS

I would like to give special thanks to the following people who have supported the Bunbury cause:

Jan and Lida Brychta, John and Norma Major, all at ESCA, Joe Cuby of EMP, Arthur Cooke, David Emery and Frances Jennings of the *Daily Express*, Ivo Tennent of *The Times*, David Welch, Charles Randall and Brendan Gallagher of the *Daily Telegraph,* Barry Brennan and John Pollard of the *Hendon Times*, *The Cricketer* Magazine, Alan Coates of McVities, George Davison of KP Foods, Mark Dubery of Brooke Bond, Barry Evans, Gerry Golding of British Gas, Paul Revell of Phileas Fogg, Lord Sam Vestey, James Sunley, Nicky Oppenheimer, Jim Pearson at Nike, Richard Little of Texaco, John Morgan of Lombard North Central Finance, David Cowham of the First National Bank, Lynn Wilson of Wilcon Homes, John Brookes and Richard Webster of Sun Life of Canada, Mike Powell of Saab City Ltd, Ron Hobson of NCP, Dr Martens, Geoff Jackson of The Halifax Building Society, Patrick Shervington of the Lords Taverners, Rory Bremner, Andrew Varley of Next Directory, Bob Godfrey Films, Mike Knowles, The Milk Marketing Board, Ian Radley of Cambridge Industries, Phillip Henson of Patrick Int. Transport, Duncan Fearnley, David Rees, Bill Archer, Teddy Markwick, Vimto, Macenzie Baird of the Walgrave Group Ltd, Vic Lewis, Roy Burns, Nick Leigh, Ian Botham, Viv Richards, Eric Clapton, George Harrison, Elton John, Gary Lineker, Bill Wyman, Peter Scudamore, John Keeble, John Altman, Dexters, Martin Sorrell of WPP, Gerry Waller, Graham Morris, Andy Sinton, Gary Headley, MCC, The TCCB, Mike Beer of Abbey National Homes, David Capel, Ian Groves, Hitachi, David Hobbs, Robin Smith, David Gower, Neal Foulds, A T Rose, Adrian Houston, John Murphy of Joe's Basement, David Clark of Infocheck, Chris Turner, Peter Hook, Dave Crowe, Charles Lock, R Mohan, Mahinda Wijesinghe, Gary Mason, Zak Syed, Michael Owen-Smith, Tony Cozier, Dave Hardy, Dick Ashby, Roger Forrester, David Hill, ex-Head of Sky Sports, Diana Keen, David Roberts, Pippa Dyson, Dennis Lillee, Michael Holding, John Holt, John Bent of Anglo American Eyewear, Yorkshire Television, Capital Radio, Grahame Dene, Mike Read, Richard Groves, Douglas Osborne, Joel Garner, Jim Alldis, Mike Milton, Finchley CC and to all those who have appeared at the Bunbury Festival and for the EMP Bunbury X1. Also Eddie Bell, Nick Wells, Liz Dean, Bev Speight, Debby Kayser and all at HarperCollins.

Thanks to Barry Gibb, the Musical Director of the Bunburys, for his time and genius.

Special thanks to David Betteridge, for his superb photography, and Allsport for their continued support.